You Want Me To Know What?

by Terry Powell

This book is geared to young teens. Though it is designed for personal reading pleasure and profit, it is also designed for group study. A 13-session *Leader's Guide* based on this book is also available from Harvest Publications.

harvest publications
Arlington Heights, Illinois

This book replaces an earlier paperback, titled *Bible Doctrine,* published by Harvest Publications. All the subjects covered in *Bible Doctrine*—plus several additional topics—are covered in *You Want Me To Know What?*

Design: Dale Janzen

CONTENTS

GIFT - Gary Lampton 11/11/2024

1

WHAT ARE YOU "BECOMING"?

Ken was only six years old. On his way to try ice skating for the first time, he passed a smaller rink. He immediately turned and asked, "What are they doing out there, dad?"

"They're playing a game called *hockey*," his dad replied.

"*I* want to play that game!" Ken announced. Knowing Ken had never been on ice skates, his dad wisely said, "First, let's learn how to skate."

That first time on the ice was something else! It's a good thing six year olds don't have far to fall. Ken spent more time picking himself up off the ice than standing on his skates. Winter and skating were soon over. With Spring came Ken's interest in baseball and other things. Spring slipped into summer, and summer into Fall. Then, without any previous discussion, Ken announced again, "Don't forget, dad. I want to play hockey."

Ken and his dad drove to the Park District office to officially sign Ken up for a "squirts" league hockey team. Ken could hardly wait for that first practice session. When the time finally arrived, Ken proudly slipped into his "Bombers" team jersey, laced up his skates, and made his wobbly way to the rink. His mom and dad, like other proud and interested parents, stood by the side of the rink to watch. It was awful! Ken was one of the worst skaters on the team. Despite his constant slipping, falling, and thrashing of arms, he managed to last through that first practice. And the next one, and the next. . . . and the next.

Then it was game time. Though he was one of the least-skilled players on the Bombers, he hung in there all winter. He saw some game action, too, because it was a league rule that every team member had to play at least one minute per period, or three minutes each game. Every chance he had, Ken also went to the rink for extra practice. By the end of this first season, he could at least skate well.

Between his first hockey season and the next Fall, not much was said about hockey. But when it came time to sign up for the "Squirts" again, Ken announced, "Don't forget, dad. I want to play hockey." Once more, Ken and his dad stood in line at the Park District office. And again, Ken was assigned to the Bombers.

That second season, Ken's dad and mom didn't attend the pre-season practice sessions, so when they attended the first game, they were pleasantly surprised. Ken had learned to play hockey! That winter he was the scoring leader not only for his team, but for the whole "squirt" league. Ken became a member of the league all-stars. All the way up through his high school years, he represented his community on traveling hockey teams. In high school, he made the metropolitan league all-star team. As a senior, besides being team captain, he received a scholarship to play collegiate hockey.

In case you haven't guessed it by now, Ken is my son. I've seen him go through the process of trying on skates for the very first time, to starting for his university hockey team. Yes, I've watched him become a hockey player.

Now this book isn't about hockey. But it is about "becoming." It's a book about "starting out" and "finishing up." It's a book that helps you move from the very first, and possibly unsure, steps of the Christian life to become all that God wants you to be. When I think of how Ken learned to play hockey, and compare it to the way we learn to live life God's way, I think of these words:

"His (God's) divine power has given us everything we need for life and godliness through our knowledge of him who called us by his own glory and goodness. Through these he has given us very great and precious promises (in His Word, the Bible) so that through them you may participate in the divine nature and escape the corruption in the world caused by evil desires" (2 Peter 1:3-4).

It's my prayer that as you read this book, you will listen to its instruction like a player listens to his coach. . . . and that you will put that instruction into practice and "become" the person God wants you to be.

So study hard! When you do, you'll find the answer to the question, "You want me to know WHAT?"

Dr. L. Ted Johnson, Executive Secretary
Educational Ministries
Baptist General Conference

2

FIRST CLASS MAIL FROM: GOD TO: YOU

SUCCESS.

Everyone wants to experience it.

But what kind of person do we have to be – what do we have to do – before we can be called "successful"? Where is the key that unlocks the door to success? Why do some people become successful and others don't?

To answer these questions, let's decide what we mean by the word "success." To many people, success is having lots of money, popularity, good looking physical appearance, athletic ability, grades, or student government positions. If our folks don't earn a big salary . . . if we aren't part of the "in" crowd at school . . . if we aren't a Mr. or Miss America look-alike . . . if we can't ring the hoop from 20 feet . . . or if we don't make the honor roll, in the eyes of the world, we're failures.

God defines success differently, though. To Him, our success hinges on whether or not we've entered a relationship with Jesus Christ; the kind of character qualities we display; how well we relate to others; and whether or not we're growing spiritually and using the abilities He has given us. Even if we don't meet some of the world's standards of success, we can be successful in God's eyes and our lives can count for something.

No matter whose definition we adopt, success isn't automatic. There are certain routes to follow and other routes to avoid. There are secrets or formulas that we must uncover and apply.

God says that success depends on what we do with His written word, the Bible. God has given only two promises of success. In each case, the formula is the same. He told Joshua, "Do not let this Book of the Law depart from your mouth; meditate on it day and night so that you may be careful to do everything written in it. Then you will be prosperous and successful" (Josh. 1:8). Also, Psalm 1:3 says this about the individual who knows and obeys the content of Scripture: "He is like a tree planted by streams of water, which yields its fruit in season and whose leaf does not wither. *Whatever he does prospers.*"

After reading the next few pages, you'll understand *why* success depends so much upon what we do with God's Word. This chapter tackles these questions: How is the Bible different from other books? Why did God give us the Bible? What can regular Bible study do for me? What are some obstacles to Bible study? What are some tips and tools to help me get more out of passages I read?

GETTING TO KNOW YOU

How do companions at school or church get to know you? How do they find out which desserts and TV shows you enjoy? Which teachers you'll try to avoid next year? What you dream about doing in the future?

They may pick up a few facts about you from others, but most of their information comes first-hand, directly from you. They get to know you well only because you choose to reveal information about yourself.

"To reveal" means to tell or to show others information that otherwise they wouldn't have. In its noun form, what we tell or show others is called a "revelation." That's a term we use for the Bible. It's one way in which God reveals information about Himself. (He has also revealed Himself through the life and work of Jesus Christ, and through nature.)

All religions except Christianity began with some attempt by man to find or to explain God. But Christianity began with *God's attempt to reach man!* Primarily through His written Word and Jesus Christ, God chose to reveal truth about Himself, the origin of the universe, man's nature, how the world will end, and so forth. Without His deliberate revelation, we couldn't know God or understand His plans.

Providing the Bible is God's way of communicating with us. It shows His keen interest in developing a relationship with individual human beings.

BANK ON IT!

Over 800,000,000 persons claim to follow the Bible's teachings. Ministers in the United States will preach between two and three billion sermons this year, using the Bible as their major source. More than 40,000,000 learners will participate in over one and one-half billion Bible lessons in Sunday School. They'll study the Bible's 66 separate books, written by more than 40 different human authors over a period of 1500 years.

Why do we pay so much attention to the Bible? We believe it's the only book ever written that was *inspired by God.* The Bible began in the mind of God, not the mind of men. The word "inspiration," as applied to the Bible, literally means that its words were "breathed out by God." Paul told Timothy, "All Scripture is *God-breathed*" (2 Tim. 3:16). In the book of Revelation, John told his readers that the Holy Spirit controlled his writing (Rev. 1:10-11).

God spoke directly to a few human authors. Moses, who wrote the first five books of the Old Testament, is an example. Others jotted down what they saw happen or what others told them, and God kept them from making errors.

Old Testament authors used the Hebrew language. New Testament words were penned in Greek. Before printing was invented, scribes copied and recopied the original manuscripts by hand many times. A few centuries ago, scholars began translating the ancient Hebrew and Greek words into more modern languages, such as German, Latin and English. A "translation" of the Bible is the result of transferring its content from the words of one language to the words of another language. No matter what modern language we print the Bible in, the words mean the same as the original Hebrew or Greek. If it weren't for translations, we'd have to learn Hebrew and Greek to understand the Bible!

Because its words came from God, we can trust the teaching of the Bible.

ON PURPOSE

When you write a letter or create an essay for a class assignment, you have a purpose in mind, a reason for writing. Every writer wants his words to accomplish something. Textbook authors want to inform the reader on a particular subject. Comic strip authors work with the aim of entertaining readers, or making them laugh. Newspaper editors write opinion columns to encourage readers to accept their viewpoints on social or political issues.

When He inspired men to write the books of the Bible, God also had purposes in mind. We can put these broad purposes in the form of results that God wants to accomplish through the Bible.

First, *God's Word can turn us away from sin.* Jeremiah 26:2-3 is one of many passages that reflect this purpose. Jeremiah served as God's prophet. In his day, the people of Judah openly disobeyed God and worshipped idols. God told Jeremiah, "stand in the courtyard of the Lord's house and speak to all the people of the towns of Judah who care to worship in the house of the Lord. Tell them everything I command you; do not omit a word. *Perhaps they will listen and each will turn from his evil way."*

When a non-Christian reads Scripture, he comes across verses that warn him of sin's consequence. He discovers that he needs forgiveness. For we who have received Jesus as Saviour, reading the Bible makes us sensitive to unconfessed sin and gives us a desire to admit them to God. The first few Old

Testament books served this purpose in David's life. To the Lord he remarked, "I have hidden your word in my heart that I might not sin against you" (Ps. 119:11).

Second, *the Bible points us to Jesus Christ by explaining who He is and why He came.* Throughout the whole Bible, Jesus gets top billing. Old Testament authors predicted His life, death and resurrection. Jesus Himself insisted that the Old Testament spoke of Him (Luke 24:44-46). The Gospels (Matthew, Mark, Luke and John) record Jesus' teachings and describe His deeds. Other New Testament books explain the significance of Jesus' life and record experiences of first-century believers who worshipped Him.

Third, *God's Word encourages us to enter a personal relationship with Christ.* To know facts about Jesus isn't enough. What matters is what we do with the information about Him. John wrote his Gospel so readers would receive Jesus as the Son of God (John 20:31). He drafted three letters – I, II and III John – to deepen his readers' relationship with Jesus (1 John 1:3).

Fourth, *Scripture provides laws and principles to guide us in day-to-day living.* Through direct instruction and through the experiences of people it portrays, the Bible offers insights for effective relationships, decision-making, problem-solving, and Christian service efforts. "All Scripture is God-breathed and is useful for teaching, rebuking, correcting, and training in righteousness, so that the man of God may be thoroughly equipped for every good work" (2 Tim. 3:16-17).

One of the verses just quoted – 2 Timothy 3:16 –

gives us a good handle on what personal Bible study can do for us. By reading His Word, we discover . . .

- what God wants us to KNOW
- what God wants us to STOP
- how God wants us to CHANGE
- how God wants us to LIVE.

Now let's move from the broad purposes of the Bible to more specific rewards it offers readers. . . .

LIFE CHANGING

The Bible isn't an outdated, mystical, far-from-the-nuts-and-bolts-of-life piece of literature. Reading its pages has practical value. God's Spirit works through His written words to make a difference in whoever takes them seriously.

When a man I know was in high school, an accident killed his 15-year-old sister. A few hours later, his mom led the family in a study of God's love and faithfulness from Romans 8. Their time of study and prayer didn't instantly erase their pain. But 30 years later, the girl's brother clearly remembers the supernatural support found that evening.

A fellow named Ty became more consistent in his quiet times after he experienced the value of memorizing Scripture. "Back in high school there was this one guy who really irritated me. He could get under my skin for no good reason, and a lot of times I felt like telling him to hang it. I was sure the Bible would have something to help me in a time like that, but the Bible wasn't around."

Ty started memorizing Scripture so he'd have it when he needed it. Before long, meeting his "friend" in the hall, chunks of 1 Corinthians 13 would pop into his mind. "Love is patient, love is kind . . . not proud." The power of the Bible kept him from a major blowup. Ty says his memory work "gives the Holy Spirit something to work with at the times when I really need it."

The Bible itself lists potential rewards for its readers. Here are just a few of the life-changing results that God produces in people through His Word:

- gives joy   Ps. 19:8; 119:14, 92, 111; James 1:25
- gives peace   Ps. 119:165
- enables us to overcome temptation   Ps. 119:9, 11; Matt. 4:1-11
- gives wisdom (equips us to make decisions, choose between right/wrong activities, etc.)   Ps. 19:7; 119:24, 66, 98-100, 104-105, 130, 133, 169
- encourages/comforts (boosts our spirits when we feel down)   Ps. 19:7; Ps. 119:25, 28, 50, 52
- keeps us close to the Lord by making us aware of sin   Heb. 4:12
- warns us of sin's negative consequences   Ps. 19:11
- causes us to hate sin and creates in us a desire to please God   Ps. 119:128

LIGHT UP YOUR LIFE!

"Aha! I've got it!"

"That's it. . . . Now I understand!"

"Of course. Why didn't I think of that before?"

We use expressions like these whenever a bright idea pops into our head, or when the fuzz in our mind clears and a solution to a problem suddenly appears. On TV or in print, you've probably seen the symbol of a turned-on light bulb representing this event in the mind. The bulb conveys the idea of a truth or solution suddenly flashing on, providing light to an otherwise darkened mind.

A big word that describes this experience is "illumination." The word means "a supplying of light; a clarification or explanation of something." We use the term "illumination" to explain an important truth about the relationship of a reader to the Bible. We can understand and think of life areas in which we need to apply its teaching because the Holy Spirit *illuminates* our minds. He turns on the light bulb in our minds and causes Bible content to come alive for us. He sheds light on passages that otherwise leave us in the dark.

Before He left earth for heaven, Jesus promised "When he, the Spirit of truth, comes, *he* will guide you into all truth" (John 16:13). The Apostle Paul stressed our dependence on the Holy Spirit and explained why the non-Christian has a harder time understanding Scripture: "No one knows the thoughts of God except the Spirit of God. We have not received the spirit of the world but the Spirit who is from God, that we may understand what God has freely given us. . . . The man without the Spirit does not accept the things that come from the Spirit of God, for they are foolishness to him, and he cannot understand them, because they are spiritually discerned" (1 Cor. 2:11-12, 14).

Realizing our need for illumination reminds us to pray before reading Scripture or participating in a Bible study. Like David, we can ask the Lord to speak personally to us in the passage. He prayed, "Open my eyes that I may see wonderful things in your law" (Ps. 119:18).

STARVATION DIET?

We call the Bible "spiritual food." Munching on its morsels of truth results in spiritual growth just as swallowing meat, vegetables, and fruit aids physical development. If we turned down *all* meals and snacks, within a few days we'd be walking zombies, sapped of energy and effectiveness. That's why we seldom skip a meal.

It's common, though, to go for long periods of time without *spiritual* food. Day after day, we starve ourselves, knowing we *should* take nourishment, yet pushing God's menu aside. An evangelist recently asked hundreds of Christian young people if they had a daily time of prayer and Bible reading. Can you guess the response? *Only three percent said they did!*

Why is spiritual starvation such a big problem? Satan fights to keep us away from God's Word. Other things in our schedule always seem more pressing. Some sections are hard to understand, so we get frustrated. We miss a scheduled devotional time once, and it keeps happening. And deep down inside we really wonder if reading the Bible will make a difference in the nitty-gritty of school, sports, and family situations.

What obstacles most often keep *you* from God's Word? Talk to the Lord about these matters. Ask for His help in overcoming these things. Do *you* want to experience the potential benefits described earlier? Will *you* be a part of the 97% who fail to experience God's best because they snub His word? Or will *you* be among the 3% who make Bible study a habit?

A PEEK AT THE MENU

Set a goal of reading Scripture for 7 minutes a day. Setting your goals too high – 30 to 60 minutes a day, for instance – makes failure more likely and tends to discourage you.

Where do you start? Read through the Gospel of Mark, or an easy-to-grasp letter such as Philippians, a small chunk at a time. Or probe a passage that speaks directly to a need or problem you have.

If you feel uptight or hassled. . . . Philippians 4

If guilt feelings weigh you down. . . . Psalm 51; 1 John 1

If you're being tempted. . . . Matthew 4:1-11; James 1:1-16; Hebrews 4:14-16; 1 Cor. 10:13

If you have an overbearing problem. . . . Hebrews 12:4-17

If you feel worthless or unloved. . . . Romans 5:1-10; Psalm 139:1-18

If you have decisions to make. . . .Psalm 37:1-7, 23-25; Proverbs 3:5-7

If you're having trouble with mom or dad. . . . Proverbs 31:10-31; Ephesians 6:1-3

If there's friction in personal relationships at school. . . . 1 Corinthians 13:1-7; 1 John 2:1-11

Whatever passage you select, here are easy-to-follow steps for having a personal Bible study time:

STEPS FOR P.B.S.

PRAY: Before you start reading, ask God to teach you truths from His Word that can help you.

READ: Read the section of Scripture three times.

    1st – a quick, general reading

    2nd – look for main ideas or teachings

3rd—look for things that mean something to you personally

APPLY: Use a pen and paper, and start your own *P.B.S.* (personal Bible study) *Notebook*. As you look for truths to apply or obey, write down what you find, using the S.P.A.C.E. method.

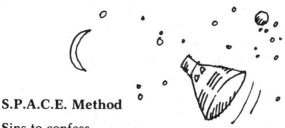

S.P.A.C.E. Method

Sins to confess.
   (Things I am doing wrong.)
Promises to claim.
   (What God says He will do for me.)
Actions to avoid.
   (Warnings not to do certain things.)
Commands to obey
   (Things God tells me to do.)
Examples to follow.
   (Something done by someone else, that I
   should also do.)

Or instead of the *S.P.A.C.E.* method, you may find it easier to use four questions based on 2 Timothy 3:16. Keep these questions in front of you as you read a passage:

• What does God want me to KNOW?
• What does God want me to STOP?
• How does God want me to CHANGE?
• How does God want me to LIVE?

A few years ago in Boston, the bodies of two elderly women were discovered in their small apartment. They had died a few days earlier. An autopsy revealed that malnutrition—poor nourishment resulting from a lack of food or improper diet —caused the deaths. But hidden in the mattresses and sewn up in pillows and draperies was nearly $200,000 in cash! The ladies died because they didn't use what they had available to meet their daily need for food.

Let's avoid *spiritual* malnutrition by adding God's Word to our daily diet.

3

AN INSIDE LOOK
AT GOD THE FATHER

(by God the Father)

Movie stars, famous athletes, politicians, and other persons in the public eye often write *autobiographies.* An autobiography is a book a person writes about himself. An autobiography describes the author's past experiences, likes and dislikes, character qualities, future goals — whatever the author wishes to reveal about himself.

Normally, we can depend on an autobiography to be accurate. After all, who is more qualified to write the life story of a person than the person himself! Writing his own book keeps a person from being misquoted. Twenty other people may have twenty different theories about that famous individual's background, feelings, and goals. Yet only one source has "inside information." That source is the famous person himself.

In one sense, the Bible is *God's* autobiography. In chapter 2 you learned that God worked through human authors to write it. Among other things, both the Old and New Testaments introduce us to God: His experiences in history, His character qualities, His thoughts, His feelings, His goals for man and the world.

Because God Himself wrote it, the Bible is our best source for information about God. There are lots of theories which try to explain the existence, nature, and work of God. Most of these views of God differ dramatically from Christian belief. The different ideas about God are almost enough to confuse us. . . . until we remember that God has written an autobiography. There *is* reliable information about Him! Christianity is different from other religions because it's based on what God has said about Himself – not on what men think about Him.

What we learn in this chapter on the doctrine of God is straight from His autobiography. We can bank on what God says about Himself.

SUPERHERO, OR . . .

Superman, Batman, Green Lantern, Flash and Wonder Woman are among the members of the Justice League of America, a make-believe crime-fighting organization made popular by TV and comic books. Too often our ideas about God are so shallow that we view Him as a fellow Justice Leaguer: a superhero who only shows up when there's trouble, who's out to get the bad guys.

But God is so much more. . . .

PERSONALITY PLUS

God is a *person*.

A person differs from things and animals. A person has what's called "self-consciousness." That means he can think about himself and use his mind to make decisions. In addition to thinking and choosing, a person has the capacity to feel and communicate with others.

We know God is a person because we are made "in His image" (in some ways like Him: Genesis 1:27). And since we can think, choose, feel, and communicate, then God must have these capacities in the most perfect and complete sense.

We can't label God an "It." He isn't the mysterious, impersonal "Force" of Star Wars fame. Instead, He's the only perfect personality.

He's different than every other person, though. He's a "Spirit" (John 4:24). Put simply, that means He exists as a Person *without a physical body*. The four-year-old girl was correct when she explained God to her brother by saying, "You can't see Him— He's *clear!*"

To imagine a person without a body is hard for us. We're tied to the way things are on earth. But this is one of many truths about God which doesn't fit the mold of routine thinking. Let's get used to thinking about God in wide-open terms.

HOW OLD IS GOD?

As I said earlier, some truths about God boggle our minds.

For instance, we can't assign an age to God. Not even 99,000,000,000,000 years! He never had a beginning! He has always existed and He will always exist. He's *eternal*, which means "without beginning, without end." In our existence, time has starting and stopping points. God, though, doesn't go by our clocks and calendars. According to Psalm 90:2, "Before the mountains were born or you brought forth the earth and the world, from everlasting to everlasting, You are God."

Also, God isn't handcuffed by human weaknesses or limitations. He's *infinite*, or unlimited in all His ways. Psalm 147:5 declares, "Great is our Lord and mighty in power; his understanding has no limit." What follows are three ways in which He is infinite.

First, He isn't boxed in by space. He can be in many places at the same time. This ability is called His "omnipresence." David acknowledged this unique quality in Psalm 139:7-10:

Where can I go from Your Spirit?
Where can I flee from your presence?
If I go up to the heavens, you are there;
If I make my bed in the depths, you are there.
If I rise on the wings of the dawn,
If I settle on the far side of the sea,
Even there your hand will guide me,
your right hand will hold me fast.

Second, His knowledge has no limits. He could score "100" on any history quiz. He's aware of every thought that has entered your mind today. He knows who will win the Super Bowl next year, and the exact number of people who will attend your high school graduation ceremonies. The big word assigned to this quality is "omniscience." "Oh, the depth of the riches of the wisdom and knowledge of God! How unsearchable His judgments" (Rom. 11:33).

Third, no superhero of TV or comic book fame can match His power. He's omnipotent, or *all*-powerful. When we ask Him for something, He may say "I won't." (He knows that some things we ask for aren't, in the long run, good for us.) But He'll never say "I can't!" The prophet Jeremiah, awed by God's creative powers, understood this divine quality: "Ah, Sovereign Lord, you have made the heavens and the earth by your great power and outstretched arm. *Nothing is too hard for you*" (Jer. 32:17).

WHAT'S HE LIKE?

A few words that describe God can be lumped together as "moral qualities." God is . . .

TRUTHFUL. Paul called Him a God "who does not lie" (Titus 1:2).

JUST. He's always fair. When circumstances turn sour, we tend to blame God and question His justice. He uses even negative situations, though, for our good. He sees circumstances from a different perspective, and never acts in an unloving way toward us. "The Lord . . . is righteous; He does no wrong. Morning by morning He dispenses His justice, and every new day He does not fail" (Zephaniah 3:20).

LOVING. A ninth-grader wrote this definition of love: "Love is a feeling you feel when you feel you have to have a feeling." To God, though, love is more than a giddy feeling. He expresses His love primarily through actions. "God is love. This is how God showed His love among us: He sent His one and only Son into the world that we might live through Him. This is love: not that we loved God, but that He loved us. . . ." (1 John 4:8-10).

GOOD. A simple but popular chorus sung in many youth group gatherings is GOD IS SO GOOD. The first stanza goes;

> God is so good,
> God is so good,
> God is so good,
> He's so good to me.

This chorus is based on Psalm 119:68, part of a poem addressed to God: "You are good, and what you do is good."

HOLY. The term "holy" turns some people off. We call someone who thinks he's spiritually above everyone else a "holy joe." We say he has a "holier-than-thou" attitude.

God, though, never pretends to be someone or something He isn't. He *alone* deserves the tag "holy." He's morally pure and perfect. God's holiness made Jesus' death on the cross necessary. Because He's holy, He hates sin. Sin cannot go unpunished. Jesus took the punishment we deserve.

As God Himself put it in a message to Israel, "I, the Lord, am holy" (Leviticus 20:26).

THE ONE AND ONLY

Here's another mind-stretching truth. There's only *one* God, yet He exists in *three different Persons:* God the Father, God the Son (Jesus Christ), and God the Holy Spirit. (The subject of this chapter is God the Father.)

Moses told Israel, "The Lord our God, the Lord is *one*" (Deut. 6:4). Yet the Father, Son, and Holy Spirit are all clearly called "God" in the Bible. In 2 Corinthians 13:14, all three are mentioned in a single sentence: "May the grace of the *Lord Jesus Christ,* and the love of *God,* and the fellowship of the *Holy Spirit* be with you all."

That's why you've heard God referred to as a

"Trinity." The fact that there's only one God is called His *unity*. The hard-to-figure-out truth that He exists in three Persons is called His *tri-unity*, or trinity ("tri" means "three").

If you could fully understand and explain the doctrine of the Trinity, you'd be world-famous among Christians of all denominations! Your picture would dot the cover of Christian magazines. You'd be in big demand as a Bible conference speaker. For the idea of *"three persons, yet still only one God"* is a mystery, beyond the human mind's ability to understand.

The following sketch doesn't clear up the mystery, but perhaps it can summarize what I've said about the Trinity. (Also see the chapters in this book on Jesus Christ and the Holy Spirit.)

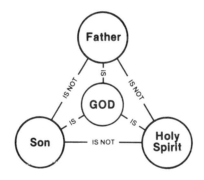

SO WHAT?

"What difference should it make?"

"So what?"

"I understand what you're saying, but what does it mean *to me?*"

Those are healthy kinds of questions to ask about Bible truths. The purpose of learning Bible content isn't to set a Ripley's BELIEVE IT OR NOT record for the number of religious facts crammed into one's head. We can know a lot *about* God, make A-pluses on Bible quizzes, and still miss out on a personal relationship *with* God.

The information in the Bible should draw us closer to God, and enable us to please Him in our daily lives. In other words, Bible content is *useful for living.* It's something we should experience, not just memorize.

Consider the descriptions of God I've outlined in this chapter. How is it helpful to know that He's personal, eternal, all-knowing, all-powerful, truthful, loving, and so forth? What difference should these qualities make in our lives?

Here are a few "so whats" to roll around in your mind:

Since God is *loving* and *fair* . . .

Why do we worry or complain when things get tough? Is such a God out to get us? Can't He be trusted even in the worst of circumstances?

Since God is *truthful* . . .

Is there ever a good reason to doubt His promises in the Bible? Doesn't it make sense to dig into His Word and discover what His promises are?

Since God is *personal* . . .

He desires person-to-person contact with us. Isn't *His* desire for a close relationship—the fact that *He* gets something out of time we spend with Him—a good reason to pray and read His Word? That *we* benefit from so-called "devotions" isn't the only reason for praying and reading the Bible. Think of it – a personal God wants to spend time with us!

Since God is *holy* and hates sin . . .

Why do we sometimes have such a casual attitude toward wrong-doing? Why do we "flirt" with sin as if it weren't a serious matter? Shouldn't His holiness keep us from sinning, or make us want to confess sins as soon as we're aware of them? "Just as he who called you is holy, so be holy in all you do" (1 Pet. 1:15).

Since God is *all-powerful* . . .

Why do we ask Him for and expect Him to do so little? Believing this about God should make us pray boldly and more often. He "is able to do immeasurably more than all we ask or imagine, according to his power that is at work within us" (Eph. 3:20).

Since God is *all-knowing* . . .

What's the use of trying to give Him a "snow job" when we pray? Why try to keep from Him the secret sins, the hidden hurts and desires? He already knows about them! When we see this truth, we're free to be honest with God in our prayers. "Let us then approach the throne of grace with confidence, so that we may receive mercy and find grace to help us in our time of need" (Heb. 4:16).

These applications of God's qualities are merely thought-starters. Can you think of other differences the descriptions of God should make in our lives?

THANK-YOU NOTE

To praise God means to honor and thank Him for both *who He is* and *what He does.* When we tell Him thanks, it's usually for something He has done for us. Here's your chance to praise Him *just for being Him.*

Imagine you're sending a thank-you note to God the Father. Look over the various qualities of God in this chapter. Then complete the thank-you card below by writing a paragraph to God. In your paragraph, tell God which one of His qualities means most to you, and why.

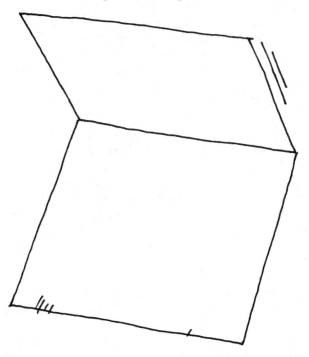

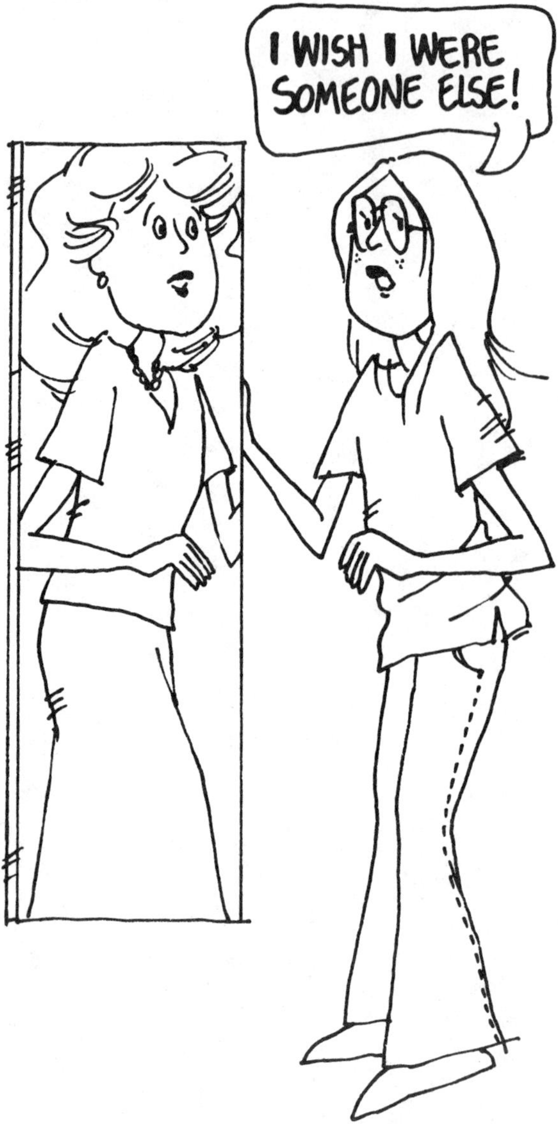
I WISH I WERE SOMEONE ELSE!

4

IF CHARLIE BROWN ONLY KNEW

Rubbish or Royalty?

Why is the Charlie Brown comic strip called "Peanuts"?

The word "peanuts" stands for more than the shelled nuts we devour. Many people use the term to describe something that's small, unimportant, or useless. If your dad calls his salary "peanuts," he's saying that it's a small amount, not enough to keep up with rising prices. When I pitched for a Little League team, we nicknamed our second baseman "Peanuts." He was the smallest player on the team.

I don't think the comic strip is called "Peanuts" though, because Charlie Brown is physically small. Perhaps it's so named because Charlie Brown feels like "peanuts." He has a hard time liking himself. He constantly criticizes himself because his teams can't win a ball game, or because he can't get a date with the little red-haired girl. An "I'll-never-amount-to-anything" attitude weighs him down. He thinks he's worthless or unimportant to persons around him. Charlie Brown suffers from what is called an "inferiority complex," or negative self-image.

You probably don't have all of Charlie Brown's hang-ups. But at times, perhaps you, too, feel like "peanuts." Do you ever feel like making any of these comments?

"I get mad at myself a lot."

"Sometimes I doubt my value as a person. I'm just one tiny speck in a world populated by billions of people!"

"It bothers me to think that I'm not as smart or as good-looking as my friends."

"I feel that God is disappointed in me because I'm not real talented or spiritual."

"I have a feeling that others won't like me if they get to know me."

"When I stare into a mirror, I wish I were somebody else!"

Believe it or not, the key to a healthy self-image is understanding Bible truths. For instance, consider what the Bible teaches about man. The Bible says both good and bad things about us. Yet the facts of this doctrine combat the worthless, purposeless feelings which often plague us.

What follows are basic truths about man from the Bible. Each truth shows how *God* sees man.

If Charlie Brown only knew these facts, perhaps he wouldn't feel like "peanuts."

GOD'S MASTERPIECE

Our existence in the world is *not* an accident. We aren't products of chance. Instead, we're products of God's creative mind. He intentionally planned the creation of mankind. To put it another way, we existed in the mind of God before we were born!

According to Genesis 1:27, "God created man in his own image, *in the image of God* he created him; male and female he created them." The fact that He created man "in His image" shows our specialness to God. Put simply, this means we're like God in some ways, but unlike Him in other ways. Like God, we can think, feel, and make decisions. Unlike God, our personalities exist within a physical body. We're limited by time and space.

God also created nature and the animal kingdom. But only man is made in God's image. Animals don't have what is called "self-consciousness." They can't reason in the same way humans can nor think about the existence of God. David understood that man is "God's Masterpiece" – His most important creation. He wrote;

> "What is man that you are mindful of him,
> the son of man that you care for him? You
> made him a little lower than the heavenly
> beings and crowned him with glory and
> honor. You made him rule over the works
> of your hands; You put everything under
> his feet: all flocks and herds, and the beasts
> of the field, the birds of the air, and the fish
> of the sea, all that swim the paths of the
> seas" (Ps. 8:4-8).

Just as He made man different from animals, God created every individual somewhat different from all other persons. We aren't all Xerox copies of Adam! The lyrics of a well-known Christian song ring true: "He made me special, *I'm the only one of my kind."*

To evaluate a work of art – a painting, novel,

sculpture, etc. — critics don't compare it to other works of art. Why? It's a unique one-of-a-kind creation. They determine its value by examinig its own features, in light of the reputation of its creator.

Ephesians 2:10 claims, "We are *God's workmanship.*" This verse portrays God as an artist, and man as His "work of art," or creative expression. Similarly, what we're worth isn't based on how we compare with others. How our muscles, looks and brains measure up to others has nothing whatsoever to do with our value as persons. The world often judges us by these standards. The truth, though, is that we're worthwhile because of *who we are:* products of God's imagination, created in His own image.

He used poor English grammar, but one person correctly summarized it this way: "God made *me* . . . and God don't make no junk!"

CREATED "WONDERFULLY COMPLEX"

The human body is made up of many chemical elements. About 70% of your body is water. About 3% is nitrogen. Someone has estimated that the human body contains:

- enough sulphur to rid a dog of fleas
- enough lime to whitewash a chicken coop
- enough fat for six bars of soap
- enough iron for a few dozen nails
- enough phosphorus for 20 boxes of matches
- enough magnesium for one dose of Milk of Magnesia
- enough sugar for 10 cups of coffee
- enough potassium to explode a toy cannon
- enough salt for 20 spoonfuls

The breakdown shows how physically complex and detailed God made us. David put it this way: "You created my inmost being; you knit me together in my mother's womb. I praise you because I am fearfully and wonderfully made; your works are wonderful, I know that full well. My frame was not hidden from you when I was made in the secret place. When I was woven together in the depths of the earth, your eyes saw my unformed body" (Ps. 139:13-16a).

We're more than mere physical creatures, though. God designed us with features which make us superior to animals:

- a *soul* and *spirit* as well as *body* (1 Thess. 5:23)
- a *mind,* an ability to think and to reason (Phil. 4:8; Isa. 1:18)
- *emotions*, the capacity to feel (Rom. 12:15)
- a *will,* an ability to make choices (Deut. 30:19; Joshua 24:15)
- a *conscience,* a sense of right and wrong (Acts 24:16; 1 Tim. 1:5)

Everyone of us is a unique combination of the "dust of the earth" and "the breath of God" (Gen. 2:7). The total value of the material or physical part of man is only a few dollars. But we're worth more than the price our chemical elements would bring on today's market. It's the part we can't see – the spiritual part – of our being that makes us priceless.

CREATED FOR A PURPOSE

A man spent months inventing a machine. The machine had all sorts of knobs, gadgets, and moving parts. When he plugged it into the electrical outlet in the wall, it ran beautifully: *Whrr-Tonka,*

Whrr-tonka . . .

A friend of the inventor who saw the machine asked, "What does your new creation do?"

"What do you mean?" the inventor replied.

"I mean, why did you make this machine? What do you intend for it to accomplish? Does it make rubber balls, popsicle sticks, or what?"

"Uh . . . it doesn't *do* anything," said the inventor, "It just runs, I guess."

Despite all his efforts, the machine is worthless to the inventor. Who wants a machine that runs, but doesn't *do* anything?!

God didn't make the inventor's mistake. When he created man, he had purposes in mind for him. First, He intended for human beings to enjoy a personal relationship with their Creator. God "wants all men to be saved and to come to a knowledge of the truth" (1 Tim. 2:4). Second, God planned for persons who love Him to represent Him in the world, among people who don't love Him. No matter what vocation we enter, He wants to use *us* to share the message of Jesus Christ with others. "You will be My witnesses," Jesus declared. As Paul put it in Ephesians 2:10, "We are God's workmanship, created in Christ Jesus to do good works, which God prepared in advance for us to do."

To help us serve Him, God has given every believer at least one special ability (1 Pet. 4:10). Each of us has the responsibility to discover and to use this so-called "spiritual gift." Would God give us such a big responsibility if He thought we were "peanuts"?

And there's more! God's plan for *your* life is unique, unlike His plan for any other person He has created. Before you were born, God saw all the days of your earthly life, He knew ahead of time what He wanted you to be and to do. David wrote "All the days ordained for me were written in your book before one of them came to be" (Ps. 139:16).

TARGET OF GOD'S THOUGHTS

When you have a close friend, you spend a lot of time thinking about this person. When the friend is away on vacation, you miss him. During the school year, you call him on the phone to go over homework or rap about a ball game. When he's sick, you take books and assignments by his house so he won't fall behind on school work. Your thoughts about this person give him worth or value.

Here's why we should never question our value to the Lord: "How precious it is, Lord, to realize that you are thinking about me constantly! I can't even count how many times a day your thoughts turn toward me" (Ps. 139:17-18, LB).

TARGET OF GOD'S LOVE

What a rosy picture of man so far.

We're "God's masterpiece," created in some ways like God Himself. Unlike animals, we have a spiritual nature. We'll live on after our current bodies die. We have the capacity to think, to feel, and to choose. God plans our lives for us and gives us meaningful work to accomplish. And He constantly thinks about us!

But strangely enough, the greatest proof of our value lies in the bleakest truth about man.

Beginning with Adam and Eve, we've used our decision-making ability to rebel against our

Creator. What the Bible calls "sin" – defying God's laws and falling short of God's goals for us – has spoiled the perfect creation of God. Every person has what's called a "sinful nature," a tendency to do wrong rather than what's right. As Jeremiah described it, "the heart is deceitful above all things and beyond cure. Who can understand it?" (Jer. 17:9). Paul added, "All have sinned and come short of the glory of God" (Rom. 3:23).

Sin limits our ability to think and to understand: "The god of this age has blinded the minds of unbelievers, so that they cannot see the light of the gospel of the glory of Christ, who is the image of God" (2 Cor. 4:4). Sin damages our emotions to the extent that we can't trust them. We have positive feelings when we should have negative ones: "This is the verdict: Light has come into the world, but men loved darkness instead of light because their deeds were evil" (John 3:19). Sin warps our conscience, or blots out the sense of right and wrong: "To the pure, all things are pure, but to those who are corrupted and do not believe, nothing is pure. In fact, both their minds and consciences are corrupted" (Titus 1:15). It weakens the will, or limits our ability to choose what we know is right: "I know that nothing good lives in me, that is, in my sinful nature. For I have the desire to do what is good, but I cannot carry it out. For what I do is not the good I want to do; no, the evil I do not want to do – this I keep on doing. Now if I do what I do not want to do, it is no longer I who do it, but it is sin living in me that does it" (Rom. 7:18-20). Since God is sinless, our disobedience drives a wedge between Him and us.

An unknown author who understood this negative view of man wrote:

"If man should ever dwell on the moon
There's one thing that is clear;
He'll ruin everything up there,
Just like he has down here!"

"But some persons aren't as bad as others," you may be thinking. That's true. Yet spiritually speaking, we're still in the same boat.

An elderly lady and a teenage boy came to a bridgeless stream of water. The lady tried to jump the short span but landed with a splash in the middle of the stream. The teen boasted that he could jump over it. He took a long run and a big leap. He sailed farther than the lady, yet fell one foot short of the bank and got soaked! Similarly, some individuals surpass others in good deeds and moral excellence. Yet everybody still falls short of God's standard of perfection.

If Charlie Brown were reading this, he'd sigh "Good grief!" about now. What an unlovely portrait of man! How can the fact of our sinful nature lead us to the greatest proof of our value?

Here's how. God shows the depth of His love for man by loving us inspite of our sin. Though man deserves the death penalty, God has acted to restore fellowship and give man a new nature through the work of Jesus Christ. "This is how God showed his love among us: He sent His one and only Son into the world that we might live through him. This is love: not that we loved God, but that He loved us and sent his Son as an atoning sacrifice for our sins" (1 John 4:9-10). Paul stressed, "God demonstrates His own love for us in this: While we were still sinners, Christ died for us" (Rom. 5:8).

We who have received Jesus as Saviour are *God's property*. We've been "bought at a price" (1 Cor. 6:20). God paid "top dollar" for us . . . His cost was the agonizing death of Jesus Christ on the cross.

A businessman told me, "Any product is as valuable as the price someone is willing to pay for it." *Imagine: we're worth the price of God's own Son!*

God wouldn't die for "peanuts," would he? If Charlie Brown only knew. . . .

5

MORE THAN A HISTORY-MAKING HERO

He was born in an obscure village, the child of a peasant woman. He grew up in still another village, where He worked in a carpenter's shop till he was thirty. Then for three years he traveled around as a preacher.

He never wrote a book. He never held an office. He never had a family or owned a house. He didn't go to college. He never visited a big city. He never traveled two hundred miles from the place where He was born. He did none of the things that we think make a person great.

He had no credentials – things that made Him important in the eyes of people – but himself.

He was only thirty-three when the public opinion turned against him. His friends ran away. He was turned over to his enemies and went through the mockery of a trial. He was nailed to a cross between two thieves. While he was dying, his executioners gambled for his clothing, the only property he had on earth. When he was dead he was laid in a borrowed grave through the pity of a friend.

Nineteen centuries have come and gone, and today he is the central figure of the human race and the leader of mankind's progress. All the armies that ever marched, all the navies that ever sailed, all the legislatures that ever sat, all the presidents that were ever elected, put together, have not affected the life of man on earth as much as that one solitary life.

You just read a well-known review of the life of Jesus Christ, titled "One Solitary Life." As the last paragraph points out, He has been the most influential person in the history of the world.

If He's all that important, isn't He worth learning more about? After all, He made some pretty bold claims about who He was and why He came to earth. A lot of Christians have a shallow understanding of Jesus Christ. And the truth is, *a lot of people who say they don't believe in Him know very little about Him!* Like the girl on page 46, they don't have enough information to make an intelligent decision *for* or *against* Jesus. And that kind of person doesn't deserve much respect.

Who was Jesus Christ? What was His unique purpose in history? What difference should the facts we uncover about Him make in our daily living?

This chapter wrestles with those questions.

JESUS – A HUMAN BEING

Jesus wasn't a ghost-like figure, or a supernatural force from outer space that temporarily occupied a human body. He was 100% man – a flesh-and-blood carpenter with bulging biceps and a sweaty brow. What follows are proofs or evidence of His humanity. As one first-grade girl put it, Jesus was God "with a man's skin on."

Jesus had a physical human body. That body was subject to physical limitations—even death.

Key phrases from Philippians 2:5-8 point this out: "being made *in human likeness,*" "being found *in appearance as a man,*" and "became *obedient to death.*"

Like every other human being, Jesus' body developed for nine months before birth within his human mother. What made his birth different was that God Himself—not a human father—was responsible for the conception of life within Mary. Yet His delivery in the Bethlehem stable and process of growth during childhood was like that of His boyhood playmates (Luke 1-2). Jesus wasn't a Bionic Boy, nor did He remove His Clark Kent disguise when a superhero was needed.

• He had to have rest and sleep (Matthew 8:24; John 4:6).

• He couldn't skip meals without getting hungry (Matthew 4:2).

• Hanging on a cross in the hot sun made Him thirsty (John 19:28).

Jesus experienced emotions common to all human beings.

• He had deep affection for other people (John 11:3, 36).

• He got angry (John 2:13-16; Mark 3:5).

• His sadness over others' grief (John 11:32-35) and sins (Luke 19:41-42) brought Him to tears.

• He felt troubled, weighted down by pressures, the night before His death on the cross (Mark 14:32-36).

Though He never gave in to them, Jesus was the

target of temptations from Satan (Matthew 4:1-11; Hebrews 2:18, 4:15).

JESUS—GOD HIMSELF!

No matter how great He was, if Jesus Christ were *only* a man, He wouldn't deserve our worship. He'd be no different than other founders of world religions such as Buddha and Mohammed, whose bodies have decayed in their graves.

Sure, it's hard to understand *how*, but Jesus Christ was fully *man* and fully *God*. Paul called Jesus, "the image of the invisible God" (Col. 1:15).

Think about the following evidences, which point to Jesus' identity as God in human form.

Jesus Christ existed before He was conceived and born as a human being. This truth is often called the "pre-existence" of Jesus. Like God the Father, Jesus is eternal. Among other things, that means Jesus Christ never had a beginning! That boggles the mind, for we limit our concept of Jesus to the historical person who lived in the first century.

But Jesus has always been alongside God the Father (John 1:1-3). Jesus was involved in the creation of the world (Col. 1:16). And He made the unusual claim, "Before Abraham was born, I am" (John 8:58). The Jewish leaders around Him knew that was Jesus' way of claiming to be God, for they threatened to stone Him (John 8:59).

Jesus insisted with His words that He was God. John emphasized, "He was even calling God His own Father, making himself equal with God" (John 5:18). Jesus told a crowd of unbelieving Jews, "I and the Father are one" (John 10:30). During His trial, the high priest said to Him, "I urge you under oath by the living God: Tell us if you are the Christ, the Son of God." Jesus answered, "Yes, it is as you say" (Matt. 26:63-64). His enemies' blood pressure skyrocketed because He claimed to be God (John 19:7).

According to several religious cults on the scene today, Jesus never claimed to be God. When they read the Bible, members of these cults must skip verses like the ones you just read!

Jesus demonstrated by His actions that He was God.

•He forgave individuals of their sins, something which the Old Testament says only *God* has the authority to do (Mark 2:8-10; Luke 19:1-10).

•He performed miracles, acts of power far beyond the natural ability of human beings. John called Jesus' miracles "signs," or ways of showing the public who He was. No mere man could have raised Lazarus from the dead (John 11), healed the man blind since birth (John 9), or fed thousands with one serving of bread and fish (John 6)!

•For thirty-three years, He lived a perfect, sinless life. He wasn't hampered by a "sinful" nature which is common to every other human being.

Living with a person day and night for a period of time gives you plenty of chances to see his or her bad as well as good side. Who knows *your* faults better than your parents, or brothers and sisters? That's why we can believe the New Testament authors when they call Jesus sinless. The same men who traveled, ate, and worked with Him for three years—who had every opportunity to see His weaknesses—called Him "Saviour," "Master," and "Lord." In their writings, both John and Peter called Jesus perfect (1 John 3:5; 1 Peter 2:22).

The Apostle Paul labeled Him "God." In a letter, he referred to Jesus as "being in very nature God" (Phil. 2:6).

Even demons—Satanic forces that occupied and controlled persons—recognized Jesus as divine. After Jesus launched His public ministry, the first one to identify Him as God was an evil spirit. In Capernaum, a demon cried out from a man, "I know who you are—the Holy One of God!" (Mark 1:24). The same thing happened in Gerasenes, when an evil spirit screamed, "What do you want with me, Son of the Most High God?" (Mark 5:7).

Jesus' resurrection from the dead proves He was God. Jesus' resurrection isn't something we have to cross our fingers about and *hope* really happened. The historical evidence for it would raise any doubter's eyebrows.

After Jesus' death on the cross, over five hundred people saw Him alive, including the twelve disciples, His half-brother, James, and Paul (1 Cor. 15:3-8). He made at least ten different appearances in bodily form after His death, spread out over a forty day period. Only eyeball-to-eyeball contact with a *risen* Jesus converted Paul from a Christian-hater to a Christian minister (Acts 9), and changed Peter from a scared, wobbly-kneed follower to a bold witness who stood up to enemies of Christ (compare Matt. 26:69-75 with Acts 4:18-20). The book of Acts tells how unbelievers jailed and killed many followers of Jesus. That proves Jesus' followers didn't hide His body or make up a story about Him rising from the dead. They wouldn't have risked their lives for Someone whom they knew was still in a grave!

JESUS – RECORD-BREAKING RANSOM

BANKER'S WIFE HELD FOR $1,000,000 RANSOM!

Chances are you've read headlines like this, or seen TV shows in which the "bad guys" kidnap an individual, then demand money for his or her safe release. The money paid to the kidnappers for the captive's release is called the "ransom."

Jesus used this word when He described why He came to earth. He "did not come to be served, but to serve, and to give his life as a *ransom* for many" (Mark 10:45). Jesus knew that sin has us handcuffed. By dying on the cross, He paid the necessary price to set us free from sin's control. Writing to believers in Corinth, Paul explained their salvation by stating, "You were bought at a price" (1 Cor. 6:20). That price was the death of Jesus Christ.

What Jesus did for us is too big to fit into the definition of one word, though. Let's put a couple more words under the microscope of our minds. What follows are simple definitions of two words which often bounce off our ears in church meetings.

Reconciliation. To "reconcile" means to settle differences between two persons, to bring them together again in a peaceful, friendly relationship. Beginning with Adam and Eve, every member of the human race has turned away from God and broken His laws for living. Sin separates us from God, who remains holy and perfect. The penalty for sin is death (Rom. 6:23), but Jesus took the rap and died in our place. That's why He's called a "sacrifice" for our sins (1 John 4:9-10). When we pray to receive Him as personal Saviour, we become *reconciled* to God. Paul wrote, "If, when we were God's enemies, we were reconciled to him through the death of his Son, how much more, having been reconciled, shall we be saved through his life (Rom. 5:10).

Justification. According to Webster's Dictionary, to "justify" means "to show to be right, to free from blame or guilt." When we trust Jesus as our Saviour, we are instantly and automatically "justified" before God ("free from blame or guilt"). As Paul put it, "Since we have been justified through faith, we have peace with God through our Lord Jesus Christ" (Rom. 5:1). Justification means there is no longer a blemish on our record. God is no longer angry at us, and we can relax in His love. "There is now no condemnation for those who are in Christ Jesus" (Rom. 8:1).

(For a more detailed explanation of why Jesus had to die on the cross, read the chapter titled "A Word To Be Experienced.")

Are "ransom," "reconciliation," and "justification" still merely big churchy words to you? Or do they describe what has happened in your life? What have *you* decided about Jesus' claim to be God? How have *you* responded to what He did for you on the cross?

If you've chosen to reject Jesus Christ, you have something in common with every other non-Christian who has ever lived. When Jesus Christ returns, *everyone* will fall at His feet and agree that He is God (Phil. 2:10-11). But at that time, it'll be too late to enter into a relationship with Him and enjoy His companionship in heaven.

When will *you* recognize Him as "lord." Sooner
. . . or *later?*

6

A WORD TO BE EXPERIENCED

A habit that he knew was wrong bothered Mark. Every time he yielded to this sin, he felt frustrated and anxious. But no matter how hard he tried, he couldn't muster enough strength to say no. It seemed as if some force were alive inside him, keeping him from doing the right thing. He felt powerless, guilty, like a slave to some unseen power.

Mark wrote a poem about sin's impact on his life:

Sin is flirty. It keeps begging for my attention.
Sin is smart. It knows when and where to hit.
Sin is noisy. I can't turn down its volume.
Sin is like alcohol. It always leaves a hangover.
Sin is strong. I can't overcome it.
Sin is heavy. It has me weighted down with guilt.

Mark isn't an isolated case. Everyone experiences the impact of sin. Your folks can't read the newspaper or see the six o'clock network news on TV without realizing that there's something dreadfully wrong with man's nature. Wars, murders, rapes, robberies, cheating, lying—sin makes headlines daily! Our personal wrestling matches with wrongdoing, as well as social conditions, illustrate the truth of God's Word:

"The heart is deceitful above all things and beyond cure. Who can understand it?" (Jer. 17:9). "All have sinned and fall short of the glory of God" (Rom. 3:23).

Every individual needs a fresh start in life . . . a "happening" in which he breaks away from sin's control and receives new power to live as God intended. This remedy, or fresh start, involves entering a personal relationship with Jesus Christ. The term we use to describe this experience is *salvation*. The term means "deliverance." It suggests that we're in some type of danger and need to be snatched away, to be brought to a place of safety.

In this chapter, let's put the word "salvation" under the microscope and look closely at its meaning.

PAID IN FULL!

The disorder, pain, and imperfection of man point to one basic problem: we're separated from the One who created us. God is holy, or without sin. When the first man, Adam, decided to disobey, he was immediately cut off from a relationship with God. This "cut off from God" state, or sinful nature, was passed down through all mankind. In one sense, we've "inherited" the tendency to sin. So like Adam, in our natural condition *we're* blocked off from God.

How frustrating! We inherited a sinful nature that we didn't ask for in the first place. We're imperfect, so there's nothing we can do to get rid of this sinful nature. And because of it, we're cut off from God and sentenced to an eternity in hell! All this sounds like *bad news*!

But wait.

God, because He loves us, provided a way out through Jesus Christ. "When the right time came, the time God decided on, He sent His son, born as a Jew, to buy freedom for us who were slaves to the law so that He could adopt us as His very own sons" (Gal. 4:4-5, LB). By dying on the cross, Jesus paid the penalty for *our* sins. "God made him who had no sin to be sin for us" (2 Cor. 5:21). "It was *our* grief He bore, *our* sorrows that weighted Him down. . . . He was wounded and bruised for *our* sins. He was chastised that *we* might have peace; he was lashed – and *we* were healed! *We* are the ones who strayed away like sheep. *We,* who left God's paths to follow our own. Yet God laid on *Him* the guilt and sins of every one of *us!*"(Isa. 53:4-6, LB).

Jesus, though, didn't waste away in a grave. He came back from the dead! So He's able – as a Spirit – to step into our lives and give us a new nature which is tied in with God.

That's great, right? But did you notice something? Though Jesus took the penalty for sin that each of us should have to pay, *the individual person is not yet united with God.* Nope. We're still in the same old cut-off-from-God situation, handcuffed by our sinful natures.

Why?

Because God doesn't force His solution of salvation on us. Jesus Christ enters our lives only when we realize our need for Him and personally invite Him to come in. That's called "receiving" what He provided on the cross. God could have created us as a planet of dutiful robots, programmed to blurt out "We-love-you-God! We-love-you-God!" hundreds of times each day. But He didn't. He gave us the capacity to choose whether to go His way or our own way.

The Bible puts it this way: "If you confess with your mouth, 'Jesus Is Lord,' and believe in your heart that God raised him from the dead, you will be saved" (Rom. 10:9). Writing to believers, Paul declared, "For it is by grace you have been saved, through faith—and this is not from yourselves, it is the gift of God—not by works, so that no one can boast" (Eph. 2:8-9).

SOMETHING BEAUTIFUL...

What really happens inside a person who experiences salvation?

To answer that question, let's do some lab work on two verbs which we often read in Sunday School manuals and hear from the pulpit: *repent* and *confess*.

Literally, "to repent" means "to change one's mind." When we repent, we start thinking differently about the way we live. The negative effects of sin haunt us. Wrong behavior starts losing its appeal. Deep down inside, we're fed up with sin and yearn for life to get better.

Repentance also refers to a change in behavior. We intentionally choose to stop disobeying and start obeying the Lord. Jesus told a group of religious leaders to "produce fruit in keeping with repentance" (Matt. 3:8). He knew that a change of mind is *not* real repentance unless it leads to a change in action.

When we pray to receive Christ, we experience this change of mind, and begin the gradual process of changing our behavior.

It's important, though, to understand the difference between repenting and just "feeling sorry" for sins. Being sorry doesn't change our lives or wipe out the guilt sin causes.

Just feeling sorry means I put all the blame for my sins on myself. I mope around and put myself down. I may believe in God, but I don't trust Him to forgive my sins. I'm like the man who carried a 100-pound sack of wheat on his shoulders while riding down the road on a donkey. Somebody spotted him and asked, "Why don't you take the weight off *your* shoulders and put it on the donkey?" The rider answered, "You don't think I'm going to ask the donkey to carry all that weight, do you?"

Of course, the donkey was already bearing the weight of the sack, anyway. When I merely feel sorry for sins, it's like putting on my own back the weight and pain of sin which Jesus has already carried on the cross. When I repent, though, it's like taking the burden of sin off my back and putting it on Jesus' back. I trust His forgiveness, receive a fresh start, and feel at peace with God and myself.

The word "confess" means "to say the same thing." When we confess a sin, we agree with God's thoughts about it. We see it through His eyes, so to speak.

First, we agree that our thought or action was wrong, that it fell short of God's standard. Second, we agree that Jesus suffered the penalty for it – that God forgives and forgets about that sin.

Someone accidently spilled ink onto a lovely, expensive handerchief. An artist who saw the mess sketched a beautiful picture on the cloth and used the blotch of ink as part of the scenery. When we *repent* and *confess*, God takes the scars and confusion caused by sin and makes something beautiful out of our lives.

YOU'RE INVITED TO...

Turning down God's offer of salvation is somewhat like missing your own birthday party.

I know a young adult who has never had a surprise birthday party ... at least not one he has attended. During his senior year in college, a group of 15-20 friends bought prizes and baked a huge cake. They planned a surprise party for him, but the person assigned the task of getting him to the party location forgot to invite him! (The person was supposed to bring him to the place without telling him why.) The group enjoyed the party *without* the guest of honor. He missed all the fun, songs, games, and fellowship of close friends.

Just as *gifts* play a key role at a birthday party, salvation and its benefits are *gifts* from God. Just as *joy* describes the atmosphere of a party, Jesus promised *joy* to His followers. Just as *close friends* attend a surprise party given in your honor, a Christian can enjoy the deepest kind of companionship with others who know the same Lord. All the trappings of a party mark one's entrance into the eternal family of God. If you aren't a Christian, right now God is inviting you to attend a party, thrown in your honor.

Becoming a Christian is called a "rebirth," or a "born-again" experience. When an individual prays to receive Jesus as Saviour, he experiences his "spiritual birthday."

Don't miss your own birthday party. After all, salvation is more than a big, churchy term.

It's a *word to be experienced.*

7

LIFE AFTER REBIRTH

On a weekend retreat, the leader asked seventh and eighth graders to use pipe cleaners to illustrate or symbolize how they felt about their relationship to God. Here are a couple of the responses:

Greg bent his pipe cleaner in the shape of a yo-yo. "I'm sort of like a yo-yo," he explained. "I have an up and down Christian life. One day I feel good about my relationship with God—like He's really close, you know—then the next day I don't feel Him at all. Then I start wondering if He's real, or if I'm really a Christian. I want to feel sure about things, but I don't."

Marie also shared some doubts. With her pipe cleaner she formed a question mark. "I don't doubt that God is real," she said, "but I've been having lots of doubts about my relationship with Him. I was so young when I prayed to receive Jesus—five years old, I think—that I'm not sure I knew what I was doing."

The leader asked Marie, "What has caused you to feel this way now?"

"I guess it's because I haven't seen many changes in my life," Marie answered. "I thought things would be easier than they are."

Feelings like Greg's and Marie's are pretty common. *Interrobang,* a book by Norman Habel, includes a poem written to God that begins with these words:

"Lord, I feel like such a fool
talking to You, trying to believe.
I'm not sure if You're listening,
or laughing, or sleeping,
or if You're really there at all!"

What causes doubts about salvation and the Lord to creep into our minds? How can we be *sure* we're saved—*or can we?* What Bible truths can help us when we doubt or feel insecure in our relationship to God? What are some facts about "life after rebirth" that can keep us off a roller-coaster kind of existence?

This chapter wrestles with these questions. You won't find "pat" answers which make Christian living a breeze. But you will find nuggets of truth that can make a positive difference.

CAUSES OF DOUBT
Fickle Feelings

Sometimes we start questioning our salvation or the reality of God because *we depend too much on feelings.* Emotions are temporary and inconsistent. God gives us a wide variety of emotions, many pleasurable. But He never intended for feelings to control our behavior.

If we've sincerely prayed to receive Jesus Christ, our salvation is rooted in *fact.* Whether we feel saved or unsaved doesn't change what happened. Jesus either entered our lives or He didn't.

Let's look at this point from the opposite angle. It's possible for a person to *"feel saved"* even if he doesn't believe in Jesus Christ. But it's a matter of *fact* that he isn't! *Feelings* and *fact* don't always go together.

What would happen if, for one week, we lived entirely on the basis of how we feel. Think of the disastrous results that would have on football practices, grades at school, and relationships among brothers and sisters! What if your mom didn't "feel" like preparing meals? If your favorite disc jockey didn't "feel" like coming on the air? If the town's only heart specialist didn't "feel" like performing emergency surgery on your dad?

So pass the word: we can't always trust our feelings.

Lack of Bible knowledge

A second, but closely-related, cause of insecurity in a relationship with God is a *lack of Bible knowledge.* We can be unaware of truths that, if known, would comfort us and increase our ability to trust. The more we know about God and how He sees us as Christians, the more ammunition we have to battle doubts and Satanic lies.

Susie told a counselor, "I've prayed about a particular sin, but I still don't *feel* forgiven. Maybe God still holds that mistake against me."

The counselor read 1 John 1:9: "If we confess our sins, he is faithful and just and will forgive us our sins and purify us from all unrighteousness." He also read Titus 1:2, which clearly states that *God does not lie.* Then he asked her a question. "Which is more reliable: your feelings, which raise doubts about forgiveness; or *God's Word*, which directly states that you *are* forgiven?"

Two specific Bible verses erased Susie's uncertainty. The promises in 1 John 1:9 and Titus 1:2 assured her that she *was* saved and her sins had been forgiven.

Bible knowledge doesn't automatically change us. It's necessary to believe and to apply the information in Scripture. Yet doubts and frustration enter a blank mind quicker than a mind filled with God's Word.

Uncertainty about God's Love

"He loves me, He loves me not . . ."

Uneasiness about our relationship with God also comes *when we misunderstand the nature of His love for us.* Even after experiencing salvation, it's easy to feel unacceptable to God, to think we have to *earn* God's favor. Perhaps we think God's love for us comes and goes, depending on "how good" we've been. But Christianity is good news because it says our worth—and our acceptability before God—is not based on our own performance.

We can explain the way God loves us by defining the three kinds of love which exist in the world. "I love you *if*—" is the first type of love. This type of love says "I'll love you *if* you never hurt me, *if* you do what I say, *if* you meet my needs, etc." When a person says "I'll love you *if*—" he means "I'll love you under certain conditions."

Another kind of love is "I love you *because*—". This love says "I love you *because* you're attractive, *because* you make me happy, *because* you're popular, etc." It's the same as saying "I love you because I can find good reasons to love you."

The third type of love is "I love you *in spite of*—" or "I love you *no matter what.*" This love says, "Sure, you have faults, but I love you anyway! No matter what kind of person you are or how you treat me, I love you." This love is unconditional, unlimited and unselfish.

God loves us "in spite of." How marvelous!

Let's review for a moment. God's standard for living is perfection. No one measures up to it. We've inherited what's called a "sinful nature," which separates us from a holy God. The story sounds bleak so far, but God visited this planet in the form of Jesus Christ. Jesus paid the penalty for our errors. When we agree that He took the punishment we deserve and receive Him as Saviour, we stand forgiven of all sins—past, present, and future. When we're saved, God *forgives* us. He no longer holds our sins against us. And on the basis of Jesus' perfection, we're *justified*—made right and pure in God's eyes. Because Jesus paid the penalty for sin on the cross, God sees us and relates to us just as if we had never sinned!

Have you seen a computer with a TV-type screen being operated? When the programmer makes an error, he presses the "cancel" button. That automatically removes all information from the screen. The programmer begins his work again without trying to sort out previous mistakes. There's not even a record of the mistake—it's lost forever! That's what happens to our sins when God forgives us (Heb. 10:17). God *forgets* about sins we confess to Him. Consequences sometimes remain, but the sin is gone (Rom. 8:1).

The Bible calls Jesus our "Advocate" or "Defense Attorney." This is an important role, because Satan tries to make us feel guilty over sins we've already prayed about. He wants us to feel anxious instead of remembering God's "inspite of" love, to put the blame on ourselves instead of on Jesus.

In a book titled *Nobody's Perfect*, I explain what I do when I start feeling guilty for a sin I've already confessed:

> I picture a courtroom in heaven. I'm the defendant. Jesus is my lawyer. God sits on the judge's bench, and Satan is the prosecuting attorney. Satan has solid proof that I just broke God's law. He confidently presents his case: "OK, God, here's the Christian You said was blameless. See what he did! Are You going to let him get away with it?"
>
> Then Jesus, my Counsel, steps before the bench. "Father, You and I agreed that My death on the cross included this sin just like all the others. I've already paid the penalty for it. Terry has trusted me as His Saviour, so the sin has been placed on My account. Why should he have to stand trial for a sin I've already paid for?"
>
> Next I hear the rap of a gavel. God says, "Case dismissed!"
>
> *What love!*

Wrong View of Christian Growth

Another cause of doubting salvation is *a shallow understanding of spiritual growth.* The changes Jesus Christ produces in a person happen gradually, over a long period of time. Spiritual maturity isn't an overnight achievement. It doesn't occur automatically or with push-button ease. We skin our knees learning to "walk" in the spiritual realm, just as we did as toddlers in the physical realm.

Recently I spotted someone wearing a large button with these letters printed on it: PBPGIFWMY! "What do these letters stand for?" I asked. "Please Be Patient, God Isn't Finished With Me Yet" he answered. The button's message is based on Philippians 1:6, "He who began a good work in you will carry it on to completion until the day of Christ Jesus."

God promises to finish whatever He starts in our lives. Yet His work of changing us is a *process* that takes time. If we're so aware of our weaknesses that we feel we'll never "arrive" spiritually, let's be thankful! This inadequacy shouldn't cause us to doubt our salvation. Rather, it suggests that we really do belong to God! It shows that we're more sensitive to sin now, that the process of growth has begun, after all.

SURE THING!

What follows are Bible references and a brief summary of the message in each passage. Look up the verses. File their teaching away in your mind. The next time doubts about your salvation get you down, dip into this "mental file" and think about the truths.

These passages provide a review of this chapter, and make "life after rebirth" more enjoyable.

Revelation 3:20 Whenever a person opens the door of his life to Jesus (prays to receive Him as Saviour), Jesus says "I *will* come in!" He does *not* say, "I *might* come in."

Romans 5:1-2, 8-9; 8:1 If I've honestly prayed to receive Jesus, God has declared "peace" in our relationship. God is *not* angry at me when I fail Him, though He wants me to pray about my sins.

2 Timothy 1:12 God promises to guard or to keep what I trust Him with, and that includes my life which I turned over to Him when I prayed to receive Christ.

1 John 5:9-13; Romans 8:16-17 God's Holy Spirit lives inside me and helps convince me that my salvation experience was real. God tells me that I *can* know without a doubt that I'm saved, and it's the "inner voice" of His Spirit which witnesses to the fact.

1 John 1:9; Hebrews 8:12; 10:17-18 After I confess sins, I can *know* I'm forgiven by God because His Word insists that it is so. What the Bible says is more dependable than emotions, which sometimes cause me to feel like I'm not forgiven.

Philippians 1:6 Though I fail at times, Jesus will help me grow spiritually over the long run. He will finish what He started in my life at the moment of salvation. Failing the Lord does *not* mean I'm unsaved. It merely shows that spiritual growth takes a long time. It isn't an automatic, overnight thing.

Ephesians 2:8-9 I didn't deserve or earn salvation in the first place. God gave it to me as a *free gift*. That's why I don't lose my salvation whenever I slip and disobey the Lord. Disobeying could cause me to lose my salvation *only* if I got salvation through being good.

2 Corinthians 5:17; 1 John 2:3-6 Though I mature over a long period of time rather than instantly, if I'm saved it will show up in the way I think, act, and feel. I'll see changes in my life. I'll have a greater desire to obey the Lord. Wrong things I enjoyed as a non-Christian won't mean as much to me.

8

WHAT'S A "HOLY SPIRIT"?

Look over the following list. What do the items have in common?

battery

wind

clean-up hitter at the plate

electricity

Holy Spirit

Each item is a *source of power.*

Just as a cassette recorder needs electric current or batteries to make it work . . .

Just as a kite needs a blast of wind to send it higher in the sky . . .

Just as a bat needs the grip of a muscular hitter to blast a baseball over the fence . . .

A Christian needs a source of power much stronger than himself in order to obey God and live an effective Christian life. In this chapter, we'll learn more about the Holy Spirit and how He gives us the power to live the kind of life Jesus wants us to live.

HOLY WHO?

What comes to mind when you read or hear the

title "Holy Spirit"?

Do you picutre a clean-living spook whose home address is somewhere in heaven? Or a mysterious impersonal "Force" that serves the same purpose as Popeye's spinach and temporarily gives people super strength?

Forget those kind of ideas. The Holy Spirit is not a "what" or an "it." He's a "Who"—a *Person!* He's *God Himself!*

The *one God* in whom Christians believe exists in *three persons*: God the Father; God the Son—Jesus Christ; and God the Holy Spirit. (This hard-to-understand, but important teaching about God is called the "Trinity.")

An episode from early church history directly shows that the Holy Spirit is God. Ananias and Sapphira were found guilty hiding money that belonged to the Lord. Peter said to them, "How is it that Satan has so filled your heart that you have *lied to the Holy Spirit* and have kept for yourself some of the money you received for the land? *You have not lied to men but to God*" (Acts 5:3-4).

Since He's God, the Holy Spirit has all the qualities or characteristics of God. He has always existed. Unlike human beings, His existence does *not* depend on a body. That's why He can be everywhere at the same time (Ps. 139:7-10). Like God the Father and Jesus Christ, the Holy Spirit knows everything, and is all-powerful.

John 14:16-17 shows how personal and important the Holy Spirit is. Knowing He would soon leave His disciples and return to heaven, Jesus promised, "I will ask the Father, and He will give you another Counselor to be with you forever—the

Spirit of truth. The world cannot accept him, because it neither sees him nor knows him. But you know him, for he lives with you and will be in you." Here the word Jesus used to describe the Holy Spirit is translated "Counselor." Literally, the word means, "one who is called alongside to help."

What follows are other proofs, or evidences, that the Holy Spirit is a *Person* rather than an "it."

•Jesus and New Testament writers used *personal pronouns (He, Him)* when they talked about the Holy Spirit.

•The Holy Spirit can *speak*, or communicate personally to men and women. He gave Philip orders to approach a chariot and witness to an official (Acts 8:29). He spoke to small groups of believers (Rev. 2:7). Normally, the Holy Spirit doesn't speak out loud to individuals. Instead, He communicates with us in a clear, yet hard-to-explain way through our inner thoughts and convictions. Most often, He "speaks" to our hearts as we pray and read the Bible.

•The Holy Spirit has emotions. He can be *grieved* (Eph. 4:30) and *insulted* (Heb. 10:29) by the words and actions of people.

Now you know what to say if anybody ever asks, "What's a *Holy Spirit?*"

HARD WORKER!

The Holy Spirit has led a busy life.

He gave God the Father and Jesus Christ a helping hand in the creation of the earth (Gen. 1:2). He often gave leaders in the Old Testament special ability to do their work. For instance, He came upon David when he was anointed king of Israel (1

Sam. 16:13). Turning to the New Testament, it was the Holy Spirit who made it possible for Mary, a virgin, to give birth to Jesus (Luke 1:35). When Jesus was baptized, the Holy Spirit took the form of a dove to show Jesus' connection with God (Matt. 3:16). And Jesus relied on the Holy Spirit's power to perform miracles.

Not long after Jesus left earth and returned to heaven, a turning point came in the history of Christianity and the role of the Holy Spirit. Acts 2 describes the events which occurred when the Holy Spirit was sent to earth *to live inside Christians.* Before that day, He was sort of like "outside help" who sometimes came upon believers. He related to believers only when God had special tasks for them to do. Ever since, though, the Holy Spirit has entered a person's life the moment he prays to receive Jesus Christ as Saviour. Paul wrote, "Don't you know that you yourselves are God's temple and that God's Spirit lives in you?" (1 Cor. 3:16)

The next section tells what the Holy Spirit does after He enters a person's life.

CHRISTIANS UNDER CONSTRUCTION

Near a section of highway that's being repaired, you may see a sign that reads CAUTION: CONSTRUCTION WORK AHEAD. Every Christian could wear a similar sign around his neck: CAUTION: HOLY SPIRIT AT WORK! It's God the Holy Spirit who wants to do "construction work" in our lives so we'll grow spiritually and serve the Lord effectively. What follows are various ways He wants to work in and for us.

•*The Holy Spirit constantly reminds us that we have*

a relationship with Jesus Christ. After we pray to receive Christ as Saviour, at times we get discouraged and wonder whether or not we're really "saved." The Holy Spirit reminds us that we belong to the Lord, even when we don't *feel* like it. Paul put it this way: "His Holy Spirit speaks to us deep in our hearts, and tells us that we really are God's children" (Rom. 8:16, LB).

•*The Holy Spirit makes us aware of the wrongs we do and shows us areas in which we need to obey the Lord* (John 16:8). At a department store, Keith stuffed a ballpoint pen into his pocket and left without paying. He felt proud and excited because the store employees didn't catch him. Two weeks later, though, his Sunday School lesson was on the subject of honesty. Along with other Bible verses, his class studied Ephesians 4:28: "He who has been stealing must steal no longer." For the first time, he began to feel guilty about the pen. A few days later he admitted his theft to the store manager and paid for the pen.

This shows the work of God's Spirit to convict us, to make us uncomfortable about our sins.

•*The Holy Spirit helps us understand the Bible.* Non-Christians have a harder time understanding God's Word, because the Holy Spirit doesn't live within them. But for us, the Spirit "opens our eyes" to the thoughts of God as expressed in Scripture. "No one knows the thoughts of God except the Spirit of God. We have not received the spirit of the world but the Spirit who is from God, that we may understand what God has freely given us" (1 Cor. 2:11-12). Also, He is a Teacher who reminds us of Bible truths when we need them from day to day

(John 14:26).

•*The Holy Spirit helps us share our faith.* He's the power source who gives us the courage to witness, and who works in the non-Christian to change his mind about Jesus. Jesus promised, "You will receive power when the Holy Spirit comes on you; and you will be my witnesses" (Acts 1:8).

•*When we're not sure how to pray or what to say in prayer, the Holy Spirit communicates our deepest thoughts and feelings to the Lord.* Sometimes we have feelings or concerns about a matter, but can't find words to express them to the Lord. That's when the Holy Spirit relays to the Lord what we want to say, but can't.

What a relief! "The Holy Spirit helps us with our daily problems and in our praying. For we don't even know what we should pray for, nor how to pray as we should; but the Holy Spirit prays for us with such feeling that it cannot be expressed in words. And the Father who knows all hearts knows, of course, what the Spirit is saying as he pleads for us" (Romans 8:26-27, LB).

•*The Holy Spirit gives us special abilities so we can do God's work in this world.* These abilities are called "spiritual gifts." Every Christian has at least one (1 Pet. 4:10). A special knack for teaching, encouraging others, sharing material resources, speaking to unbelievers about Jesus, or managing other people to accomplish a project are among the gifts the Spirit gives. Other gifts are listed in Romans 12:3-8; 1 Corinthians 12:4-11; and Ephesians 4:7-13.

The Holy Spirit chooses to give different gifts to different individuals. That's why you need other

Christians, and they need you!

In the future, make it a point to learn more about "spiritual gifts." Ask the Lord to show you which gift the Spirit has given you, and how He wants you to use it. He has service opportunities reserved especially for you!

•*The Holy Spirit gives us the power to say "no" to sin and to please God in our thoughts and deeds.* What's the difference between a Christian who has the "blahs" and a Christian who seems to stay on top of things? One lives from day to day on his own power, and the other depends on God's Spirit!

Though *every* believer has the Holy Spirit, not every believer lets the Holy Spirit control him. We still have what's called a sinful nature—a tendency to do the opposite of what God wants. Every day God gives us the freedom to make right or wrong choices. We aren't created as robots, programmed to obey automatically. But if it's our honest goal to please the Lord, through His Spirit He gives us the ability to live right.

The Bible tells us to "live by the Spirit" (Gal. 5:16), "walk in the Spirit" (Gal. 5:21), and "be filled with the Spirit" (Eph. 5:18). Paul used these phrases to point out that we can't follow the Bible's instructions on our own. Trying to live the Christian life in our own strength is like relying on a V-8 engine which has four burnt cylinders. . . . we merely sputter along.

Just as the stereo needs electricity before it plays your favorite record . . .

Just as a flashlight needs a battery to produce a beam of light . . .

Just as the marathon runner needs stout muscles

to propel his legs over the 26-mile course...

We need a source of power—the Person of the Holy Spirit—to help us apply the Christian faith at school, home, and the nitty-gritty of social relationships.

FRUIT FACTORY

Few of us are *horticulturalists*. (That's a person who makes a hobby or career out of growing gardens or orchards. He knows all sorts of interesting facts about shrubs and trees.) We usually cannot identify or label a tree by inspecting its bark, or by examining the size and shape of its leaves.

During warm months of the year, though, we *can* correctly identify an apple tree, or a peach tree, or a cherry tree. Yesiree, if apples are dangling off its branches, we know it's an apple tree! (We didn't even have to go to school to learn this!) That establishes a principle: some trees are known or recognized by the fruit they bear.

According to Jesus, we're known by the kind of "fruit" we bear, too. He said that a Christian who is hooked up to the Holy Spirit will bear good fruit, but a person controlled by his own desires will bear bad fruit (Matt. 7:15-20). The "fruit" that a Spirit-controlled believer bears is the nature of Jesus Christ Himself. "The fruit of the Spirit is love, joy, peace, patience, kindness, goodness, faithfulness, gentleness, and self-control" (Gal. 5:22-23).

Use the following chart to look at *your* life in light of each of these nine qualities. Put a check mark in the appropriate column, then jot down answers to the questions. Before you begin, ask a teacher or parent to explain and illustrate each quality so you'll better understand how it shows up in a life.

FRUIT INSPECTION

When It comes to the fruit of . . .		A LOT	A LITTLE	HARDLY ANY	NONE AT ALL
LOVE	I'm bearing				
JOY	I'm bearing				
PEACE	I'm bearing				
PATIENCE	I'm bearing				
KINDNESS	I'm bearing				
GOODNESS	I'm bearing				
FAITHFULNESS	I'm bearing				
GENTLENESS	I'm bearing				
SELF-CONTROL	I'm bearing				

1. Take time right now to thank the Holy Spirit for the fruit He has produced in your life (for the qualities which you rated "A LOT" or "A LITTLE"). *He* deserves credit for these positive qualities.

2. List the fruit of the Spirit which are missing in your life (ones which you checked "HARDLY ANY" or "NONE AT ALL").

_____

_____

What is preventing God's Spirit from developing these qualities in you? Check the answers that apply in your case.

_____Not sure I'm a Christian

_____sins I haven't confessed (prayed about) . . . see 1 John 1:8-10

_____I hardly ever spend time with the Lord by reading the Bible

_____I hardly ever ask the Lord to help me please Him

_____OTHER (fill in)

_____

_____

9

LIFE IN THE FAMILY OF GOD

Many small children use hand-motions to visually illustrate the words of this poem:

"This is the church
and here is the steeple;
Open the door
and see all the people!"

What do these well-known lines teach about the word "church"? The poem describes the church as a building, a place where Christian people meet.

According to the Bible, though, the church is not a stained-glass building. Nor is it the meetings, organizations, and activities that we call "going to church." These things *do* play an important role in the life of a church. Believers need a building to meet in. Meetings enable leaders to make decisions and plan ministries that help others. The organization and activities of a particular church provide opportunities for people to study Scripture, worship God, and share Jesus Christ.

The "church," though, is *people* ... persons who have received Jesus Christ as Saviour. The word "church" literally means "called out ones" and refers to those individuals whom God has chosen to be a part of His family. In this sense, *every* Christian is part of what's called the "universal church." However, we use the word most often to refer to a "local church" – a group of persons in a particular location who meet regularly and combine their efforts to serve the Lord. A "local church" normally has appointed leaders (pastor, board members, etc.), planning committees, a statement of common beliefs, programs for Bible instruction and fellowship, and other things that make it an organization.

Why did God come up with the idea of a local church? What does He want local churches to be like and to do?

This chapter on the doctrine of the church tackles these questions and helps us see the church through His eyes.

FOREVER FAMILY

Two phrases in the New Testament which describe the church are "the household of God" and "the body of Christ." These terms point to a new and special identity which God gives every new Christian.

When an individual becomes a Christian, he belongs to *God's Family* – a large family which includes every person in the world who believes in Jesus Christ. The New Testament often uses the terms "brothers" and "sisters" to refer to other believers, to represent a *spiritual* rather than a physical relationship. When they prayed to receive Christ, Paul told the Ephesians, "You are no longer strangers to God and foreigners to heaven, but you are *members of God's very own family*, citizens of

God's country, and *you belong in God's household with every other Christian."* (Eph. 2:19, LB).

The Bible calls this family of Christians the "body of Christ." What is the meaning behind this "body of Christ" idea?

None of us is expected to make it alone as a believer. God knows that living the Christian life, sharing our faith with non-Christians, and working out our problems is far beyond our own ability. So He has provided help. He has planned for Christians to relate closely to one another and to help each other along.

In a book titled *How Do I Fit In?*, Larry Richards explains it this way: "According to the Bible, our family relationships with other Christians and our place in the family have carefully been designed to let us help and be helped. It works out much like a body works. Each part of our body has something important to contribute to the whole. Similarly, each of us as a Christian has something important to contribute to other believers' lives. And we've been given just the personalities and special abilities we need to do our helping jobs."

Paul's words to the Christians in Corinth and Rome get more specific in comparing the church to a human body:

> Our bodies have many parts, but the many parts make up only one body when they are all put together. So it is with the 'body' of Christ. Each of us is a part of the one body of Christ. Some of us are Jews, some are Gentiles, some are slaves and some are free. But the Holy Spirit has fitted us all together in one body. . . .

Yes, the body has many parts, not just one part. If the foot says, "I am not a part of the body because I am not a hand," that does not make it any less a part of the body. And what would you think if you heard an ear say, "I am not a part of the body because I am only an ear, and not an eye"? Would that make it any less a part of the body? Suppose the whole body were an eye—then how would you hear? Or if your whole body were just one big ear, how could you smell anything?

But that isn't the way God has made us. He has made many parts for our bodies and has put each part just where he wants it. What a strange thing a body would be if it had only one part! So he has made many parts, but still there is only one body.

The eye can never say to the hand, "I don't need you." The head can't say to the feet, "I don't need you."

Now here is what I am trying to say: All of you together are the one body of Christ and each one of you is a separate and necessary part of it (1 Cor. 12:12-21, 27, LB).

Just as there are many parts to our bodies, so it is with Christ's body. We are all parts of it, and it takes everyone of us to make it complete, for we each have different work to do. So we belong to each other, and each needs all the others" (Rom. 12:4-5, LB).

To help us understand what it means to act like members of a family, or parts of a body, God has given specific commands to guide our relationships. What follows are a few of these instructions.

- love one another (John 13:34-35)
- accept one another (Romans 15:7)
- serve one another with the abilities God has given us (Galatians 5:13; 1 Peter 4:10)
- honor or give value to one another (Ephesians 4:2; Colossians 3:13)
- comfort, encourage one another (1 Thessalonians 4:18)
- admonish or correct one another (Colossians 3:16; Romans 15:4)
- bear one another's burdens (Galatians 6:2)
- forgive one another (Ephesians 4:32)
- teach one another (Colossians 3:16)
- pray for one another (Ephesians 6:18)

I know . . . all this sounds rather ideal. After all, as someone has put it, *people are harder to get along with than anybody!* Even Christians get on each other's nerves. Yet the fact that we often fall short of these instructions doesn't mean we should shuck the whole idea of a local church.

No local church is perfect, because no individual who joins it is perfect. Yet the existence of local churches is still *God's* idea, not man's. The failure to live together as God intended – to experience God's ideal – merely shows that Christian maturity is not something we produce within ourselves. Only God's Spirit – not our own power – can enable us to obey the "one another" commands in day to day situations.

A church, though, isn't just another social group or country club. God has *goals* for each local church – things he wants believers to do when they meet together, and when they scatter as individuals during the week.

Let's find out what God expects of a church, and why getting involved in a local church is important to the individual believer.

VITAMIN "G"?

One of the unhappy secrets of the Christian life is this: *spiritual growth takes place over a long period of time; it isn't an automatic or overnight event.* We can't buy a bottle of "one-a-day growth pills" in a Christian bookstore, or flex bulging, supernatural biceps the day after receiving Jesus Christ.

Yet the Bible does reveal keys or means to spiritual growth. These keys to growth may be called vital experiences which God wants us to have, or spiritual disciplines which He wants us to make a part of our lives.

By examining Acts 2:42-27, we discover those things God says we need in order to grow spiritually. These verses describe the lifestyle of the first group of believers in Jerusalem.

"They devoted themselves to the apostles' teaching and to the fellowship, to the breaking of bread and to prayer. Everyone was filled with awe, and many wonders and miracles were done by the apostles. All the believers were together and had everything in common. Selling their possessions and goods, they gave to anyone as he had need. Every day they continued to meet together with glad and sincere hearts, praising God and enjoying the favor of all the people. And the Lord added to their number daily those who were being saved."

We don't have to be carbon copies of the Jerusalem Christians, yet the keys to their growth are the same ones we need today.

What follows are the involvements or commitments of those Jerusalem Christians. The thing to note is this: *the secrets to their personal spiritual growth centered on their participation with a group of believers who made up a local church.* They didn't grow in isolation from others.

So what follows are, in one sense, keys to personal growth. But in another sense, the list reveals God's goals for the corporate or group life of a local church. As an individual, I need each of the following experiences. And my local church should provide the opportunity and training for each experience.

•*Group worship of God* To worship means to concentrate on the Person of God, to remember what He is like and what He has done for us. This vital experience is seen in the church's participation in communion ("the breaking of bread"), prayer, and praise.

An individual can worship the Lord when he's alone. Yet God enjoys it when believers worship as a group, too. And He has made us so that we benefit from group worship experiences. Hearing others' songs, testimonies, and prayers increases our love and appreciation for the Lord. That's why we're instructed to meet together to worship. "Let us not give up meeting together, as some are in the habit of doing, but let us encourage one another — and all the more as you see the Day approaching" (Heb. 10:25).

•*Bible instruction* Members of the Jerusalem church "devoted themselves to the apostles' teaching." They knew that the Scriptures would bring them closer to the Lord and give them guidelines for daily living.

We can and should study God's Word in private. But to make the most of Bible study, we need others' abilities and input. Gifted teachers help us understand tough passages and show us *how* to study on our own. Hearing others share their insights on a passage makes us want to dig deeper into the Word, and nudges us to obey what we already know.

•*Close relationships with other Christians* In Acts 2, we see the "household of God" and "body of Christ" idea at work. Christians in Jerusalem weren't strangers to one another. They met together regularly—in homes as well as in the temple—for worship, instruction, and meals.

•*Every individual active in ministry* The apostles served the Lord by teaching. Others, perhaps not as skilled at talking before a group, ministered by sharing material resources with persons in need. Other chapters in the book of Acts show how believers served one another through supportive prayer, hospitality, words of encouragement, administration of church business, and so forth.

Church members didn't expect leaders like Peter to do *all* the work. They understood that Christianity isn't a spectator sport. It isn't God's plan for a majority of believers in a church to sit and watch a few others perform.

A regular customer of a small general store discovered one morning that the slow-moving clerk wasn't around.

"Where's Eddie? Is he sick?"

"Nope," replied the store owner, "He ain't working here no more."

"Do you have anyone in mind for the vacancy?" the customer asked.

"Nope. *Eddie didn't leave no vacancy!*"

That was the store owner's way of saying that Eddie hadn't done enough work to be missed. God doesn't want "Eddies" in local churches. He wants *every* Christian to find a way to serve Him. As Peter put it in a letter to local churches, "God has given each of you some special abilities; be sure to use them to help each other, passing on to others God's many kinds of blessings" (1 Pet. 4:10, LB).

•*Sharing their faith* Acts 2:47 refers to "those who were being saved." Foes of Christ tossed Peter and John into prison for witnessing, yet the number of Christians grew to about 5000 (Acts 4:1-4). Even when severe persecution of Christians began, "those who had been scattered preached the Word wherever they went" (Acts 8:4). The Christians didn't sit back, play with their halos, and neglect people who were unsaved.

A well-known Christian leader, Stuart Briscoe, has warned today's churches not to drop this commitment to witnessing:

"We sometimes think that all that really matters is that we should be good, honest, clean-living, church-going Christians. Now with all due respect that's a copout. There are going to be souls in hell who are convinced you were a good, clean-living, church-going Christian, and they'll be in hell because they never heard what Jesus Christ can do for them. I'm alarmed at the viewpoint that the sole task of the church is to turn out nice Christian people. I believe the sole task of the church is to turn out people who honestly believe they have the *only* message of hope, and they are the *only* people who have it."

To summarize, God wants persons in each local church to

•mature in worship
•receive Biblical instruction
•enjoy close relationships with one another
•use abilities and resources to minister to others
•share their faith with non-Christians.

Perhaps now we can better understand the advice in Hebrews 10:24-25: "Let us consider how we may spur one another on toward love and good deeds. Let us not give up meeting together, as some are in the habit of doing, but let us encourage one another. . . ."

One young person expressed the idea of "church" in this way:

"God created me with missing parts,
and He put those missing parts in other people!"

10

HOW DO I FIT INTO MY CHURCH?

In recent years, the sport of tennis has mushroomed in popularity. Top professionals earn millions of dollars in a year. Televised matches have made a few young racket-swingers household names. In parks and school grounds across the country, kids and adults swarm tennis courts to get a whack at the ball.

Have you ever thought about what it takes, physically, to play a good game of tennis? Your whole body gets into the act!

Your eyes stay glued to the ball as it darts back and forth across the net. Your hand firmly grips the racket. Muscles in your back, shoulders, and arm supply power for serves and volleys. Your legs zig-zag all over the court, depending on where your opponent drives the ball. The heart beats faster than usual, pumping the extra flow of blood and adrenalin required by the strenuous exercise. When you feel cocky about your lead, your vocal chords shout "40-love!" When an opponent's serve zooms toward your head at 80 m.p.h., your brain relays a message to your nervous system: *"Move*

—and hurry!"

Think about it: both seen and unseen parts of your physical body have to work together on the court. These body parts are vastly different in size, shape, and function. Each adds something unique and different to the effort of the whole body— something which no other part can offer. Yet no single part is complete in itself. What results in a coordinated body is the *combined effort* of the many parts. If any part fails to pitch in and do its job, it dramatically affects the whole body's performance.

The tennis illustration helps us understand why Paul called the local church the "body" of Christ. Every individual Christian is a *necessary* part of it. Before the local church body can do God's work effectively, every "part" must get involved and fit into the life of the group. When everybody gets into the act, the combined effort of the church is more coordinated and packs more wallop in the world.

Paul explained, "Just as each of us has one body with many members, and these members do not all have the same function, so in Christ we who are many form one body, and each member belongs to all the others" (Rom. 12:4-5). He also wrote that the church "grows and builds itself up in love *as each part does its work*" (Eph. 4:16).

What meaning does this "body of Christ" idea have for you? Precisely this: if you've received Christ as your Saviour, you are an important "part" of your local church "body." You can fit into its purpose and play an important role in its ministry *now.* Becoming more active in the life of your church will help others as well as yourself.

Here are a few ways to start "fitting in."

"Fitting in" through a right view of the church

A Christian is part of the "church" *at all times* — not just when he's inside a church building or participating in a church-sponsored program.

When we're scratching our heads over an unsolved math problem . . .

When we're cutting up a frog in biology . . .

When we're talking with friends on the school bus . . .

When we're behind 9-0 in the bottom of the seventh inning . . .

When we're mowing the lawn on Saturday morning . . .

When we're deciding who to invite to a pajama party . . .

we're living as vital parts of the body of Christ in the world!

When we grasp this truth, we understand that every part of our life and schedule is important to the Lord. If we've received Jesus as Saviour, then *all* of life becomes sacred and important. God doesn't label the time we spend at worship services and Bible studies "spiritual," and brand the other things in our schedules "unspiritual." When we attend a ball game or diagram sentences, we don't have to say, "Excuse me, Lord" . . .

The point is this: "fitting into" the church means, first of all, that *we represent the Lord and the church in every area of life.*

Paul called us "ambassadors" of Christ (2 Cor. 5:20). An ambassador is an official representative of an important ruler or organization. For instance, the United States has full-time ambassadors in most foreign countries. How these ambassadors act, speak, and think gives an impression of the United States. Foreigners may form opinions about other people in the United States based on what an ambassador says and does. In the same way, the view unbelievers have of the Lord and other Christians is shaped, in part, by what we say and do among them.

Being an ambassador is a big responsibility. That's why Scripture says, "Whatever you do, whether in word or deed, do it all in the name of the Lord Jesus" (Col. 3:17).

To sum up, it's okay to live a balanced life and enjoy a variety of experiences. But we're *full-time Christians*, and we "fit into" the church by living all the time as a representative of Jesus Christ. That's true because "church" is not a place we attend. If we know Jesus Christ, it's *who we are.*

"Fitting in" through church membership

Most local churches have a list of individuals who have officially joined. Persons on this membership roll enjoy privileges and responsibilities not available to non-members. During business meetings, they can vote on important decisions: how to most effectively reach the community for Christ; which missionaries to support; whether or not to invite a new pastor or build a new building, and so forth.

In many churches, only official members can teach classes, serve on boards, and occupy other leadership positions. Non-members who attend can take advantage of and support the church's ministries, but their participation is limited. They're a part of the local church body, but often there are fewer ways they can "fit in" and serve. Becoming a member is the ultimate way to declare, "This is *my* church!"

Joining a church is like saying, "I need the help which other people here can give me. And I want to share my abilities, time, and money to help this group of believers do the Lord's work." Church membership involves committing yourself to the *people* in the church, to the *work* of the church, and most importantly, to the *Person* of Jesus Christ.

The precise procedures and qualifications for membership differ among local churches. In all Baptist churches, however, you'll find these membership requirements:

• a personal relationship with Jesus Christ

• a verbal testimony of how you became a Christian (shared with the congregation or with a person on the Church board)

• baptism by being dipped or immersed under water

Is God's spirit telling you to speak to your parents or pastor about joining the church?

"Fitting in" through worship service attendance and participation

Many Christians have a warped view of worship. We often hear the complaint, "I didn't get anything out of the worship service today!" But what *we* get out of worship isn't the point. What matters is what *God* gets out of it! Worship is more for *God's* benefit than man's.

To worship means to honor God, to give value to Him because of *who He is* and *what He has done* for us. We express our worship through prayer, singing, sharing, listening to God's Word, and so forth. Sometimes we'll have a neat emotional experience during a worship service. Other times we won't feel a thing. But if we honestly love the Lord, even when participation in worship *seems* meaningless (or boring) to us, even then God enjoys and appreciates it!

Participating in worship is also important because it's something believers do *together*. Things like singing, praying, sharing testimonies, and taking communion *as a group* strengthens our relationships with one another in the church. It reminds us that we aren't supposed to go it alone in the Christian life. Worshipping together reminds us that other people share the same beliefs, joys, and struggles. That's why the author of Hebrews wrote, "Let us not give up meeting together, as some are in the habit of doing, but let us encourage one another" (Heb. 10:25).

What is your attitude toward your church's worship services? Do you look for excuses not to attend? Do you disturb others with excessive chatter and note-passing? I know . . . sometimes the pastor speaks over your head. What goes on often seems out of touch with *your* needs and interests. But perhaps viewing worhsip as something mostly for *God's* benefit can make a difference in your attitude.

"Fitting in" through sharing money God gives us

Everything we possess is *God's property*. Every Christian has been "bought" by God. The price He paid was the death of His Son, Jesus Christ (1 Cor.

6:19-20). That makes us *stewards* – managers, not owners – of our time, talents, bodies, money – everything! A steward is a person put in charge of managing something that belongs to someone else.

Looking at it this way, all the money we earn is *God's*. He asks us to give part of it back through the local church so others can learn about Him, and to use the rest wisely. God's Word boldly states that the smartest way to use money is to give a part of it to Christian work. Giving so others can serve God *is in itself a form of Christian service or ministry (see 2 Corinthians 8-9)*.

A giving person doesn't have to worry about having enough for himself, either. Speaking to people who share, the Bible says, "God is able to make it up to you by giving you everything you need and more, so that there will not only be enough for your own needs, but plenty left over to give joyfully to others" (2 Cor. 9:8, LB).

"Fitting in" through outreach

You hear several different terms that refer to sharing the message of Jesus Christ with other people. Terms like "witnessing," "evangelism," "sharing the gospel," and "outreach" are common. I'm using the word "outreach" because it's a general term that includes all forms of sharing Christ with others.

Outreach can take the form of *group projects* that reach unsaved persons (Christian films, evangelistic rally, retreats, visitation, etc.). Or it can take the form of personal, one-on-one sharing of an individual Christian with a non-Christian. We're "fitting into the church" when we get involved in either group or personal outreach activities.

Let's focus for a moment on personal sharing, or witnessing to unsaved persons. We sometimes think that living a good life around others is all that's needed. But effective witnessing includes *both* word-of-mouth sharing and being a good example in behavior. In high school, Jean learned this lesson the hard way: "I concentrated on living a good, silent life, hoping that through my actions alone friends would want to trust Christ. But they never brought up the subject of Jesus. They merely thought I was a 'do-gooder' since I refused to go along with some of their activities. Over a period of time our friendship weakened and they never knew I was trying to witness for Jesus through my actions. I learned that unless I talk about the gospel, my 'do-good' life only draws attention to myself."

Think of a non-Christian you care about. What is this person's attitude toward Jesus Christ? When will you have a chance to share with this person? What are some specific things that God has done in your life that you'd like to tell this person?

In the past year, in what ways have your Sunday School class or youth group tried to reach non-Christians your age? Have you pitched in and played an active role in these efforts?

There's only one way to gain the courage, confidence, and know-how to share Christ with others. That's by *doing it!*

"Fitting in" through missions

Your local church supports missionaries and mission organizations who serve the Lord throughout the world. For instance, the Baptist

General Conference denomination has both Home and World Missions departments which send and support Christian workers in the United States and overseas. By working together, the churches in our denomination can accomplish more in missions' work than any single church could by itself.

Here are a few ways members of a local congregation play a role in missions:

•Praying for the needs missionaries share in letters or visits to the church

•Giving money to meet the living and working expenses of missionaries

Most churches have a "mission budget" in which certain dollar amounts are designated for each person or organization they support. Persons in the church put money into this budget so checks can be sent out.

•Communicating directly with missionaries

You, your family, and church group can write letters or make cassette tapes to send missionaries. When you correspond, share news about your family/group, offer words that you think will encourage them, and ask questions about their schedules and responsibilities. If missionary families have children your age, start a "pen pal" relationship with them. They'll enjoy hearing from caring persons back home.

•Being open to possible missions work in the future

You aren't too young to think ahead and talk to God about ways to serve Him. Let your life be a blank sheet on which the Lord can write His will for your life. Too many of us give Him a sheet filled with *our* plans and merely ask Him to sign it!

Start now thinking about opportunities such as the URBANA missions conference and short-term mission work. URBANA, sponsored by Inter-Varsity Christian Fellowship, is held every other year in December at Urbana, Illinois. Thousands of teens and young adults come from all over the world to hear well-known speakers and participate in Bible studies on Christian service. Even youth who plan non-missionary careers attend. They learn more about needs in the world and grow spiritually by mingling for a week with other Christians.

Short-term missions work involves serving the Lord for a summer at a needy spot in the world. Numerous mission organizations sponsor youth as well as adults who want to help construct a school or church building, or assist missionaries in special outreach programs.

After all, "missionary work" is more of a lifestyle than a vocation. No matter where you live or what career you plan, you can fit into the work of the church by getting involved in missions.

FIT FOR A LIFETIME...

You're also "fitting in"

... *when you pray* for persons in your church, and for the ministries of your church. "The prayer of a righteous man is powerful and effective" (James 5:16).

... *when you speak a word of encouragement* to your parents, friends, pastor or Sunday School teacher. Knowing you appreciate them puts joy in their hearts.

... *when you discover and start using your "spiritual*

gift." Without exception, God has given *every* Christian one or more special abilities which enable him to contribute to the life and work of the church. "Each one should use whatever gift he has received to serve others" (1 Pet. 4:10). A special knack for teaching, encouraging others, sharing material resources, speaking to unbelievers about Jesus, or managing other people to accomplish a project are among the gifts the Spirit gives. You may not know right now what your gift is, but if you're willing to serve the Lord, He will reveal it to you in the years ahead.

The list of ways to fit into the church could go on and on. Applying what you've read in this chapter, though, should keep you busy for a lifetime!

11

CREATIVE REVIEWS OF HISTORY

What do the following things have in common? That is, in what way are these items alike?

American flag

wedding band

cross dangling from a necklace

an eight-sided red sign

an early-American patriot painted on a football helmet

Before reading the next paragraph, take a few minutes to think it over, and jot down your answer here:

_____

_____

Each object on the list is a *symbol*. According to the dictionary, a *symbol* is "something that stands for or suggests something else by reason of relationship, association, or resemblance." Put simply, a symbol is *a visible sign of something else.* That "something else" can be another object, an event, an institution (such as a church or school), or an idea.

The fifty stars on the American flag stand for the fifty different states in the United States. The thirteen strips represent the first thirteen states we had back in 1776 when the country was formed.

A wedding band on a person's finger says that the person is married. It symbolizes the love and lifetime commitment between two individuals. The cross is the best-known symbol of Christianity. Looking at it reminds us that Jesus died for our sins. A red, eight-sided sign is the symbol of a traffic law that means "stop." A patriot emblazoned on a football helmet stands for a particular school or professional team. Spectators associate that emblem with one school or team as opposed to another.

This chapter focuses on two activities that God wants Christians to participate in: *baptism* and the *Lord's Supper* (often called "communion"). These events are, in one sense, symbols. Like other symbols, baptism and the Lord's Supper carry a message. They are visible signs of something else. They stand for extremely important experiences and elements of the Christian faith.

Unless we understand what baptism and communion symbolize, they seem like meaningless rituals. Let's tackle a few questions about each of these churchy activities. What we learn may keep us from feeling bored during the next baptism and communion service.

MORE THAN A BIG SPLASH

What does the act of baptism symbolize? What experiences or truths does it stand for?

What makes Christian baptism a special occasion is *not* what happens to you when you're dipped into the water. Instead, baptism is special because of the story it tells. It's like giving a public testimony of something that has happened to Jesus, and to you. It's like a drama because it relates historical experiences to people who are watching.

First, *baptism symbolizes what happened to Jesus.* Referring to the content of his sermons, Paul wrote "What I received I passed on to you as of first importance: that Christ died for our sins according to the Scriptures, that he was buried, that he was raised on the third day according to the Scriptures" (1 Cor. 15:3-4).

The act of baptism is like sign language which describes the events Paul mentioned. When a pastor takes you below the water, it stands for Jesus' death and burial. His body, by being buried in a tomb, "went under" the earth. By coming up out of the water, you're representing Jesus' resurrection from the dead. *He* came up out of the grave!

Second, *baptism symbolizes what has happened to you.* Romans 6 is one of the "heavyweight" chapters in the New Testament. It's chock-full of important —yet hard-to-grasp—truths. Let's look at one key verse and discover how the act of baptism sheds some "light on the heavy." Paul remarked, "Your old sin-loving nature was buried with Him by baptism when He died, and when God the Father, with glorious power, brought Him back to life again, you were given His wonderful new life to enjoy" (Rom. 6:4, LB).

By being lowered into the water, you're saying, "I've received Jesus Christ as Saviour. I have, in effect, *died* to sin's control over my life. I want to *bury* my old way of life."

Rising from the water is a way of saying, "I want

Christ to raise me to a new, higher level of living. I want the same power that raised Him from the dead to help me in daily situations."

If you're a Christian, you can "look upon your old sin nature as dead and unresponsive to sin, and instead be alive to God, alert to Him, through Jesus Christ our Lord" (Rom. 6:11, LB).

What method or procedure do Baptist churches use to baptize an individual, and why?

Complete immersion in water! No "baptist" church pours or sprinkles water over an individual's head.

Why are Baptists so picky about *how* a person gets baptized?

For two reasons. First, only by going all the way under the water and coming out again can the act of baptism symbolize burial and resurrection (as explained earlier). Second, the Greek word which we translate "baptize" literally means "to dip or submerge."

We shouldn't snub believers who have been sprinkled instead of immersed. The different methods aren't worth quarreling over. It's helpful, though, to know the sound reasons behind your church's approach.

Do I need to be baptized before I can be saved?
NO!

As explained in the chapter titled "A Word To Be Experienced," salvation is a free gift of God. We receive it by believing Jesus was God, and praying to accept Him as Saviour. We can't *do* anything to earn salvation. It's based on what Jesus did for us.

The response to the first question in this chapter explains that baptism *follows* salvation. Baptism is a public way of informing others of your past salvation experience. That's why Baptist churches don't baptize babies. Only persons who are old enough to understand why Jesus died and to believe in Him are qualified for baptism. (This *can* include young children!)

Scripture *does* command Christians to be baptized, though. Jesus ordered His disciples to baptize new Christians as well as teach them (Matt. 28:19). And the first Christian church in Jerusalem had regular baptismal services (Acts 2:38, 41).

How many times should I be baptized?

The same number of times that Jesus died on the cross and rose from the dead. The same number of times a person is "saved."

Once!

If you're a Christian who hasn't been baptized, chat with your parents and/or pastor about it this week. Share with them *why* you want to obey Christ in this matter by explaining what you learned in this chapter.

SUPPER TIME!

Why is participation in the Lord's Supper, or communion, so important for Christians? What's the meaning behind the juice and crackers?

The night before He died, Jesus met with his disciples to eat a meal which was part of the Jewish Passover festivities. The religious events related to the annual Passover celebrated the release of Israel's people from slavery in Egypt (as described in the book of Exodus). After the meal, Jesus took a loaf of bread and gave each disciple a piece. He said, "Take and eat; this is my body" (Matt. 26:26). Next, He passed around a large cup of wine, and said, "Drink from it, all of you. This is my blood . . . which is poured out for many for the forgiveness of sins" (Matt. 26:27-28).

Jesus meant that the bread and drink were *symbols* of His body and blood. He knew ahead of time that His body would be beaten and killed. He understood that He had to receive the death penalty for *our* sins (2 Cor. 5:21). Without His death on the cross, we'd still be out in left field, spiritually speaking. We'd be separated from God — forever!

We take communion to help us remember what Jesus did for us. During that first communion service, Jesus instructed His disciples to make this ritual a part of the church's regular worship: "Do this in remembrance of me" (Luke 22:19).

Why is communion handled only in worship services when the whole church is together?

First, taking communion is a way of worshipping God. To worship God means to think about His character and deeds. We can focus attention on Him in a variety of ways in a worship service: praying, testimonies, singing, studying His Word, communion, and so forth.

Worship is something God receives from us. Why is that important to remember? *What matters about communion and other acts of worship is not what we get out of them, but what God gets out of them!* We make or hear comments like, "I didn't get anything out of the worship service today," or "Communion was a waste of time today. It didn't seem to do much for me."

Worship, though, is something *God* desires and enjoys. It's directed toward *Him* — not toward us. Sometimes we'll have a neat emotional experience as we think about God during communion. Other times we won't feel a thing. But if we participate in it because we honestly love and appreciate the Lord, it's still a meaningful act.

Second, we participate in communion corporately — as part of a large group — because it can strengthen our relationships with other Christians. Worshipping *together* reminds us that we aren't alone in trying to live the Christian life. Others share the same beliefs, the same joys, the same struggles. Communion is one of many things we do which brings us together as the "family" of God.

Before every communion service at my church, the pastor gives a brief talk. He keeps urging us to "examine ourselves." What's he talking about?

Your pastor bases his remarks on instructions Paul gave the church at Corinth.

We're warned against participating in communion in an "unworthy manner" (1 Cor. 11:27). We're instructed to "examine ourselves" before eating the bread or drinking from the cup (1 Cor. 11:28).

If we're angry or bitter toward another person . . .

If a sin has been dogging us and we haven't prayed about it . . .

If we engage in horseplay and disturb others who want to worship . . .

If we know we haven't prayed to receive Christ as Saviour . . .

then before participating, we need to settle things with the Lord. That's not like waiting until we're perfect until we take part. Instead, it means we approach a time of worship not hiding anything from the Lord and not pretending to be more "spiritual" than we really are.

Now you know . . .
Baptism is not a sanctified swimming party.
The Lord's Supper is not a Baptist burger bash.
These events are *symbols* which remind us of important experiences in our lives, and in the life of Jesus.

12

WHAT'S A "BAPTIST"?

Methodist.
Presbyterian.
Lutheran.
Church of Christ.
Evangelical Free Church.
Christian Missionary Alliance.
Mennonite.
Episcopalian.
Church of God.
Baptist.

Whew!

That's just a few of the categories or groupings of people within Christianity. Many of us can rattle off the names of six or eight different denominations quicker than we can quote John 3:16. In fact, a few of the above labels represent many different so-called denominations. Under the "Baptist" label, for instance, there's the Southern Baptist Convention, Conservative Baptists, American Baptists, the Baptist General Conference, and so on.

All Christians have a lot in common. Genuine believers attend churches in each denomination and grouping. Yet churches in one denomination are in some ways different from churches in all other denominations. Denominations may differ in some matters of belief, manner of worship, and approach to church government or organizational policy. And all denominations differ historically. That is, each group can look back to differnt persons and events that resulted in its birth and shaped its current existence.

In this chapter, we'll discuss questions like these: How are "Baptists" different? What is a "denomination"? What is the unique history of the Baptist General Conference, and what are its important ministries?

In God's eyes, persons who have received Jesus Christ are first and foremost "Christian" rather than members of a particular church or denomination. Yet it's importnat to understand our spiritual roots, to enjoy that "family feeling" and group identity with others in the Baptist General Conference.

BIRTH OF THE BAPTISTS

In Europe, back in the 1500s, the ancestors of twentieth-century Baptists were tough-minded people who weren't afraid to speak out for their beliefs. They were called "Anabaptists," which meant "*re*baptizers," or "people who baptized a second time." They earned this label by opposing the common practice of baptizing babies. They insisted that when a person accepted Jesus as Saviour, he had to be baptized *again* even if he had already been baptized as a baby.

Those believers felt that baptism was a symbol of the Christian salvation experience—a visible way to express one's faith in Jesus Christ, *not* an act that saves infants or guarantees them a permanent address in heaven. Baptism is for saved persons only, they insisted. That's why anyone baptized as a baby should be baptized again (rebaptized) after receiving Jesus Christ as Saviour.

The Anabaptists weren't just being picky about when to dip somebody in water. The deeper issue at stake was obedience to Scripture. They based their views concerning baptism and other touchy issues on the teachings of the Bible. They rebelled against established churches only when they felt Scripture was being ignored. For instance, they also spoke out against churches that allowed unbelievers to become members.

Because their views were unpopular at the time, Anabaptists were treated harshly. Members of a rival church group burned one Anabaptist leader at the stake, and drowned his wife in a river!

In 1608, the first official Baptist church was formed in Amsterdam, Holland by Christians whose beliefs had separated them from the church in England. A few decades later, Baptist work began in the United States in the Providence Colony of Rhode Island.

The chruch in the early American colonies was linked to politics and government. The government tried to control policies and beliefs of the church. (This was before the colonies declared their independence from England and before the American Constitution guaranteeing religious liberty was written.) Though they had fled England in order to enjoy religious freedom in America, many Pilgrims and Puritans wanted everybody in the colonies to join the same kind of church and live under the same religious authority.

A pastor named Roger Williams disagreed. He

said that government should *not* interfere with church life, that every colonist should have complete freedom to worship wherever and however he pleased. In 1639, Williams and ten others started the First Baptist Church in Providence, Rhode Island. Baptist colonists experienced hard times, though. For example, in the colony of Virginia parents were fined large amounts of money for refusing to have their babies baptized!

By 1800 there were 100,000 Baptists in the United States. That figure swelled to 4,000,000 in 1900 and close to 40,000,000 by 1980. Adoniram Judson, the first American foreign missionary, was a Baptist. The First Baptist Church of Philadelphia launched the first Sunday School in America in 1815. What started with a handful of persecuted believers has become a strong force in American Christianity.

The brief survey of Baptist beginnings points to several characteristics that we call "Baptist distinctives" – traits which set Baptists apart from many other church groups. The following points are true of some non-Baptist groups, too; but Baptist groups have put special emphasis on them.

Baptists stress the freedom and responsibility of every person in his relationship to Jesus Christ. God gives pastors and other leaders to teach and guide the work of local churches. Yet each individual has what's called "direct access" to God. That means every Christian can pray directly to God. He can read and understand the Bible on his own. No leader or organization has the right to exercise total control over his lifestyle and decisions. Also, every believer – not just the professionals who earn their living in Christian service — has the privilege of using his gifts and abilities for the Lord. The pastoral staff of a local church exists to help *us* serve the Lord, not to do all the work for us.

The Baptist approach to church government is congregational in form. That is, the business and policies of a local church are in the hands of its own church members. Each member has the same rights as any other. Every member can vote in a business meeting or hold office. All the members of a church — not just the Board members or pastor — can have something to say about important decisions.

Also, each local church is free from outside control. It has the right to rule itself. No denominational executive or organizational headquarters can control the policies or decisions of a Baptist church. Members of each church call their own pastor, elect their own officers, write their own membership procedures, and so forth.

Baptists believe that churches should be organizationally separate from the political government of the country. This means that the government should not interfere with or bother the religious life of churches, and that every person has the right to believe and worship as he pleases. Baptists believe in religious liberty for everyone — even Catholics, Jews, Buddhists — since no one can be forced to receive Jesus as Saviour and live for Him. On the other hand, Christians should honor the government and obey its laws unless it demands something clearly opposed to the teaching of the Bible.

TEAMWORK

Throughout history, Christian churches in various geographical locations have pooled or combined their resources and efforts to spread the gospel of Jesus Christ. They've found that working together made each church stronger and increased the total strength of all the churches. The rewards of cooperation among churches helps us understand why a number of individual churches with similar beliefs and practices form what's called a "denomination." The purpose behind denominations isn't to build walls to separate church groups from one another. Instead, when a group of churches put their ideas, manpower, and money together they're able to accomplish more than any one church could do by itself.

Your church belongs to a denominational group called the *Baptist General Conference*. Here's a definition or viewpoint to remember:

THE BAPTIST GENERAL CONFERENCE IS A FELLOWSHIP OF CHURCHES WORKING TOGETHER TO ACCOMPLISH WHAT THE CHURCHES SEPARATELY WOULD NOT BE STRONG ENOUGH TO DO.

Now let's find out more about this larger family to which your local church belongs. . . .

A BACKWARD GLANCE

The Baptist General Conference was born in August, 1852 at Rock Island, Illinois. Gustaf Palmquist, a preacher who had come to the United States from Sweden, baptized two men and a woman in a river. Five days later, this small group officially organized the first "Swedish Baptist

Church" in America.

Growth was slow at first. Yet by 1879, 65 Swedish Baptist Churches existed in the upper Midwest and Northeast sections of the country. In 1894, a revival meeting in Winnipeg led to the forming of Canada's first Swedish Baptist Church. ("Swedish Baptist" was later changed to "Baptist General Conference.")

In the 1890s and early 1900s, hundreds of thousands of people moved to the United States from European countries. This swelling immigration, plus many church revivals and lots of personal witnessing by church members, made this time period one of rapid growth for the Baptist General Conference. By 1902 we had 324 churches and almost 22,000 members. By 1985, we had over 730 churches and over 130,000 members in 14 different United States geographical districts.

UNDER THE MICROSCOPE

A closer look at the organization and ministries of the Baptist General Conference can help you understand how a lot of local churches working together can accomplish more than each church could by itself.

The prayers and financial gifts of local churches help support the work of people at the Conference's international headquarters and in the offices of each geographical district. (The international headquarters is in Arlington Heights, Illinois-a suburb of Chicago.) People who work in these offices do a variety of things to assist local churches and help spread the gospel of Jesus Christ. For instance, the Conference —

—reaches overseas with the gospel by appointing and supporting foreign missionaries

—provides expert advice, financial support, and in some cases pastoral leadership to churches just getting started (The Conference's 1985-1990 goal is to help start 150 new churches in 5 years in the United States.)

—holds seminars and writes materials to help train pastors as well as volunteer church workers

—publishes a full-length magazine, *The Standard,* which contains news and articles of interest to people in local churches

—operates camps and retreat centers where both children and adults enjoy meaningful experiences

—provides top-notch Christian education through Bethel College and Bethel Seminary

—organizes women's and men's groups which help local church people build lasting friendships and get involved in Christian service projects

—stages an annual meeting where several thousand people review the work of the Conference, and make decisions about future ministries (Members of each local church can elect delegates to attend and vote for them.)

As stated earlier, in addition to the international service center in Illinois, the Baptist General Conference has 14 geographical districts in the United States. Many of the ministries just described—especially camps and retreat centers— are the work of people who serve in district headquarters offices. It is the combined effort of local churches, district workers, and personnel at the international headquarters that accomplishes things for God.

There's a lot more to the work of the Baptist General Conference. But that gives you an idea of how much more can be accomplished when churches work together under the title of a denomination.

Now, before you turn on the TV or rush to the refrigerator for a snack, look over the last few paragraphs about the Conference's college which was mentioned earlier. There *is* life after high school – and it isn't too early for you to start thinking about it.

WHERE STUDENTS *ENJOY* SCHOOL...

Bethel College and Bethel Seminary are located on a wooded 231 acre site near St. Paul, Minnesota. The lovely campus and new buidings give a visitor a good first impression. And the more a visitor learns about these schools, the more impressed he gets!

The college was founded over 100 years ago on an idea. The idea may be stated like this: "You don't have to give up God to get a college education, nor give up a college education to stay close to God." It's a "four-year liberal arts college." That means you can attend Bethel to prepare for just about any career there is. You can choose from 28 major fields of study: business, nursing, Bible, math, art, history, physical education, music – you name it! But no matter what courses you take, you'll be taught by teachers who love Jesus Christ. You'll also take a few Bible course to help you grow as a Christian, and make friends who'll last for a lifetime.

According to a 1979 national survey, college

freshman said that they consider the five things that follow to be the most important goals in life:

•finding purpose and meaning in life
•a good marriage and family life
•strong friendships
•finding steady work
•being successful in my work

Why do over 1900 students attend Bethel each year? Because the school exists to help young people achieve every one of those five goals!

Bethel Seminary is a highly-respected graduate school where students receive a more in-depth education in Bible, and more specialized training in areas of Christian service. Most of its graduates become pastors, youth ministers, missionaries, and other full-time workers for Jesus Christ.

Your future is just around the corner. Start asking the Lord if Bethel is part of His plan for *your* life.

13

PEOPLE ARE FOREVER

Imagine that you've been granted *one wish* which will come true.

How will you use it? Will you wish for better grades? More money? More friends? Better looks? An improved curve ball or jump shot?

Maybe. But most people, if given only one wish, would probably say, *"I want to live forever!"*

In this chapter, you'll discover that "living forever" isn't a wish, but a reality. Jesus insisted that there's an existence beyond this earthly life for *everyone*, either in heaven or hell. So in one sense, *everybody will live forever.* Death is *not* the final event for either the Christian or the non-Christian.

What *does* God's Word teach about the end of the world? What is "life after death" like for the Christian? For the non-Christian? What will Jesus' return be like? When will it happen? Why is it important in the here-and-now to know what the Bible teaches about the future?

The fact that predictions of future events occupy about *one-fourth* of God's Word, and 1,800 Bible passages deal with the end of the world, make the doctrine of "last things" an important subject.

Theaters often show previews of "coming attractions"—movies scheduled for the near future. This chapter responds to the above questions and previews the "Coming Attractions" in the future of the world.

"I SHALL RETURN!" – JESUS

The Bible mentions more than one "coming" of Jesus Christ. The first, celebrated at Christmas, was his birth in Bethlehem nearly 2000 years ago. That stay lasted thirty-three years, and ended with His return-trip to heaven. And as Hebrews 9:28 points out, He has already scheduled a *second* trip; "Christ was sacrificed once to take away the sins of many people; and *he will appear a second time*, not to bear sin, but to bring salvation to those who are waiting for him."

That Bible verse says that when He returns, Christ *will bring salvation* to His followers. "But that's confusing," you may be thinking. "I thought salvation is something a person experiences in *this* life!"

You're right, but so was the writer of Hebrews. What Scripture calls "salvation" has past, present, *and* future aspects!

For those of us who have prayed to receive Christ as Saviour, salvation is a *past* event. We entered a relationship with Christ the instant we said the prayer. At that time, God forgave us of our sins, and reserved a place for us in heaven. Salvation is a *present* event because each new day, we experience God's help in our studies, work, play, and relationships. He lives within us *now*, and can give us the strength to say "no" to sin in the present moment. Salvation is a *future* event because when Jesus returns, for the first time we'll have 100% victory over sin and physical pain. Heaven is like the final act in a long play titled "Salvation."

The second time Jesus comes, He will appear *in the sky,* not on the earth. This future event is called the "rapture" of the church. It is the time when Christians who have died will be raised, and receive their new, heavenly bodies. And Christians who are still alive will be caught up with Jesus in the sky and also receive their new bodies.

People who study the Bible in order to understand the end time events arrive at several different conclusions. The following is one that many Christians believe.

While Christians are in heaven with Jesus, people left behind on earth will go through what is called the "tribulation"— a seven year period during which God judges mankind for sin. At the end of seven years, Jesus will return from heaven *with* the Christians who were previously raptured. He will defeat Satan and his forces in a battle, imprison Satan, and reign *on earth* for a period of one thousand years. At the end of the one thousand years, Satan will be loosed from his imprisonment. He will lead one last rebellion against God, but he will be defeated again and cast into a "lake of fire" forever. At this time, *unbelievers* who have died throughout history will be raised from the dead and *all* persons who have not received Jesus Christ as Saviour will be judged. Christians will be with Jesus forever, while non-Christians will live forever in hell.

Other people think these events will happen in a different order or a different way.

ONLY GOD KNOWS FOR SURE

How will Jesus return?

Will He hop a Universal Airlines flight from the Pearly Gate Jetport to Chicago's O'Hare Field? Will He save gas by hitching a ride back with an astronaut who happens to zoom through the area?

Of course, Jesus isn't limited to *our* means of travel. He won't need to rent a man-made vehicle of any kind. A close look at Scripture does reveal a few things, though, about the nature of His second coming.

Now Appearing — In Person ...

Acts 1:4-11 records Jesus' last earthly appearance before His return to heaven. He was teaching a band of followers, standing among them in a visible, bodily form, when "he was taken up before their eyes, and a cloud hid him from their sight" (Acts 1:9). His followers "were looking intently up into the sky as he was going, when suddenly two men dressed in white stood beside them. 'Men of Galilee,' they said, 'why do you stand here looking into the sky? This same Jesus, who has been taken from you into heaven, will come back *in the same way* you have seen him go into heaven'" (Acts 1:10-11).

If Jesus will return *in the same way* He left, then we know

—He'll return "in person," with what's called a "resurrected body" which will look a lot like the physical body He had as a man on earth.

—He'll appear *in the sky.* (Both Jesus and Paul pointed this out: Matthew 24:30 and 1 Thessalonians 4:16-17.)

How long does it take to twinkle your eye?
A flash of lightning travels 186,000 miles per second! Jesus compared His coming with the speed of lightning in order to say that it will be *sudden* and *instantaneous* (Matt. 24:27). Unlike the gradual, slow approach of an airplane toward an airstrip, Jesus' return will be too fast to trace on radar. As Paul described it, the events of that day will occur "in a flash, in the twinkling of an eye" (1 Cor. 15:52).

Surprise! No one knows precisely *when* Jesus will come again. Because it has been almost 2000 years since He promised to return, a lot of people say He'll *never* show up. Jesus' return will catch these people by surprise, like a burglar breaking into a house after bedtime (1 Thess. 5:2).

A few people have added their opinion to the Bible and set specific dates for Jesus' return. Early in 1979, a small colony of believers in Indiana predicted that the "end times" would begin on July 4 of that year, starting with an earthquake which would destroy the city of Chicago. July 4 did arrive with a "bang" — lots of fireworks were set off — but when it was over, Chicago was still nestled safely on the shore of Lake Michigan.

In 1975, members of a Bible study group in another mid-western state said God directly told them that the world would end within a few weeks. Parents quit their jobs, pulled their children out of public schools, stopped making payments on their houses, and separated themselves completely from the outside world. In the spring of 1976, this cluster of families was *still* waiting on the Lord — and law officers were waiting on them to pay their bills!

God doesn't want us to waste time trying to figure out the exact date. Jesus insisted. "No one knows about that day or hour, not even the angels in heaven" (Matt. 24:32). He wants us to live from day to day in such a way that we're ready, no matter when it happens.

DRIVE SLOWLY— HEAVEN CAN WAIT!

If you brainstormed for bumper sticker slogans on the end times, you might create attention-getting statements like these:

DRIVE SLOWLY— HEAVEN CAN WAIT!

JESUS MAKES DEATH A HEAVENLY EX-PERIENCE.

YES, THERE *IS* DEATH BEFORE LIFE.

Those particular slogans refer to what occurs when a person's life on earth comes to an end. Let's take an even closer look at what happens to the Christian, and to the non-Christian, when the series of end-time events start occurring.

The Christian:

When he dies, a Christian's non-material part, or soul, immediately enters the presence of Jesus Christ in another realm of existence. Jesus told one of the thieves who was crucified alongside Him, "*Today* you will be with me in paradise" (Luke 23:43). Paul said that a split second after his last heartbeat he would be "absent from the body" and "present with the Lord" (2 Cor. 5:8).

At the rapture, when Jesus comes in the sky to take Christans back to heaven with Him, God will miraculously reunite the Christian's soul (immaterial part that we can't see) and his body (material part). Paul shared encouraging news with believers in Thessalonica who were worried about the fate of Christians who die before this event. "The Lord himself will come down from heaven with a loud command, with the voice of the archangel and with the trumpet call of God, *and the dead in Christ will rise first.* After that, we who are still alive and are left will be caught up with them in the clouds to meet the Lord in the air. And so we will be with the Lord forever" (1 Thess. 4:16-17). The believer's *new* body will look like the one he had on earth, except it won't experience pain, aging or death (see 1 Cor. 15:35-56).

Every believer will also have an appointment in God's courtroom. "For we must all appear before the judgment seat of Christ, that each one may receive what is due him for the things done while in the body, whether good or bad" (2 Cor. 5:10).

Relax…God will *not* be deciding whether or not the Christian can enter heaven. That's already guaranteed. God will determine what rewards to give or withhold from each believer, depending on how he obeyed and served God on earth.

Though every person will enjoy heaven, individuals who are loyal to the Lord in this life have "extras" or "bonuses" to look forward to. God's Word doesn't give a lot of details about the Christian's lifestyle in heaven. We know, though, that it'll be more exciting than just perching on a cloud and strumming a harp for eternity! (That's *great* news for persons who can't play musical instruments!)

The non-Christian:

When a non-Christian dies, his chance for salvation ends. His soul, or non-material element, enters a place of torment. (Jesus told a story of the agony an unbelieving man experienced immediately after death. The man had a conscious existence in a place of fire — see Luke 16:19-31).

After Jesus returns, there will be a final showdown between Jesus and Satan. Jesus will toss Satan into what's called a "lake of fire" (Rev. 20:7-10). Next, the soul and body of *non-Christians* will miraculously unite again. The "unsaved dead" will rise from their graves and keep their appointments in God's courtroom. Because they rejected Christ, they'll receive the same sentence as Satan. They'll live forever in hell: a painful, endless separation from the God who created and loved them (Rev. 20:11-15).

FUTURE IN PRESENT TENSE

God wants us to "put the future into the present tense." That is, He wants us to know how we should live *now* in light of Jesus' second coming, heaven and hell, and so forth. What follows are areas of our lives directly affected by the reality of Christ's return.

1. Our eternal destiny. Two fellows, one a Christian and the other an atheist (one who says he doesn't believe in God's existence) were arguing about Christianity. They wrapped up their discussion with remarks about eternal destiny (heaven and hell). This is what the Christian said last: "If I'm wrong, it won't make much difference. I have nothing to lose. I won't face any consequences for having believed a lie. But if *you're* wrong, it makes all the difference in the world. You have *everything* to lose!"

The lyrics to a popular Christian song — "I Wish We'd All Been Ready" by Larry Norman—include these words:

"There's no time to change your mind,
The Son is come and you've been left behind."

Now is the time to make up our minds about Jesus Christ.

2. Sharing Our Faith. One of my college teachers defined *love* as "wanting what is best for another person, and helping him find it." Do we want our friends and family members to enjoy heaven—God's best—with us? Or do we want them to die as non-Christians?

What made Paul want to witness to others was his belief in Jesus' return and His judgment. He wrote, "For we must all stand before Christ to be judged and have our lives laid bare—before Him...It is because of the solemn fear of the Lord which is ever present in our minds, that we work so hard to win others" (2 Cor. 5:10-11, LB).

As a young teen, I had a crush on a school cheerleader. Between classes, I tagged behind her up and down the halls. I told friends how I felt about her, and stuffed mushy poems in her locker. Yet I didn't have the nerve to speak to her face to face. I figured she'd give me the brush-off.

Then one afternoon, when I spotted her standing alone by her locker, I overcame wobbly knees and erratic heatbeats long enough to tell her how I felt. After staring at me for a moment, she asked wide-eyed, "Why didn't you tell me this before?"

That's what some unbelievers say when they finally hear the Good News of Christ!

3. Our daily spiritual growth. Just as the news of soon-arriving guests prompts Mom to clean the house, the news of Christ's return should encourage us to keep our lives clean. Most Bible passages that talk about the end times also list what God wants us to be and to do *now,* while we're waiting, in order to grow spiritually.

• He wants us to meet others' needs by using the gifts and abilities He has given us (1 Peter 4:10-11).

• He instructs us to work hard at improving personal relationships: to love others (1 Pet. 4:8); to share our homes with them (1Pet. 4:9); to encourage them (1 Thess. 5:11); and to stop complaining against others (James 5:9).

• Being aware of a better existence ahead should help us cope with the problems and painful experiences in this life (1 Thess. 4:13-16, 18; 2 Pet. 3:17; James 5:7-8, 11).

• Knowing what's ahead should affect how we pray (1 Pet. 4:7).

• God calls for purity in our thoughts and attitudes (1 John 3:2-3).

Summing up God's goal for Christian living in the here-and-now, Peter wrote, "You ought to live holy and godly lives as you look forward to the day of God and speed its coming" (2 Pet. 3:11-12). John added "Now, dear children, continue in him, so that when he appears we may be confident and unashamed before him at his coming" (1 John 2:28).

Are *you* "putting the future into the present tense"?